C. H. SPURGEON ON PRAYER

31 BIBLICAL INSIGHTS FOR PRAYERS THAT AVAIL MUCH.

GODLIPRESS TEAM

CONTENTS

Introduction	ix
1. A CALL TO PRAYER	1
A Call	1
A Caution	2
A Command	3
Daily Reflection	4
2. ENCOURAGEMENT TO PRAY	5
Encouragement	6
Reasons	7
Daily Reflection	8
3. WHEN SHOULD WE PRAY?	9
Daily Reflection	12
4. MY HOURLY PRAYER	13
The Need	13
The Result	14
Daily Reflection	16
5. PERSONAL COMMUNION	17
Daily Reflection	20
6. PERSONAL ANSWERS	21
Daily Reflection	24
7. LEAD US NOT INTO TEMPTATION	25
Daily Reflection	28
8. LET US PRAY	29
A Touchstone	30
A Grindstone	31
A Tombstone	32
Daily Reflection	32

9. THANKSGIVING TO THE FATHER	34
Daily Reflection	36
10. PRAYING IN THE HOLY SPIRIT	38
A Test	39
A Tonic	40
A Map	40
Daily Reflection	41
11. ORDER IN PRAYER	43
Who We Address	44
Asking Specifically	45
Desiring His Will	46
Daily Reflection	46
12. BIBLICAL ARGUMENTS TO USE IN PRAYER	48
Examples of Arguments	49
Daily Reflection	51
13. THE SECRET POWER IN PRAYER	52
Daily Reflection	55
14. ESSENTIAL POINTS IN PRAYER	56
Our Place	57
Our Requirement	58
Our Assurance of an Answer	58
Daily Reflection	59
15. UNANSWERED PRAYERS	61
When Prayers Are Not Answered	62
Why Prayers Are Not Answered	63
Daily Reflection	64
16. BRIEF AND SILENT PRAYER	65
Nehemiah Prays	65
The Manner of Prayer	66
The Style of Praying	67
Daily Reflection	68
17. PRAYING AND WAITING	70
Knowing	70
Confidence	71

Conviction	72
Daily Reflection	73
18. A GOLDEN PRAYER	**75**
Daily Reflection	78
19. PRAYER MEETINGS	**79**
In the Early Church	79
Why Have Them?	80
Obstacles	81
Daily Reflection	82
20. PRAY WITHOUT CEASING	**84**
Daily Reflection	87
21. ASK AND HAVE	**88**
Daily Reflection	91
22. HINDRANCES TO PRAYER	**92**
Hindered *From* Prayer	92
Hindered *in* Prayer	93
Hindered From Effective Praying	94
Daily Reflection	95
23. KNOCK	**97**
Daily Reflection	100
24. THE PROOF OF GODLINESS	**101**
A Test	101
A Motive	102
A Time	103
Daily Reflection	104
25. HUMILITY, THE FRIEND OF PRAYER	**105**
It Is an Attitude of Prayer	105
It Is an Argument in Prayer	107
Daily Reflection	108
26. INTERCESSORY PRAYER	**109**
Daily Reflection	112
27. TRUE PRAYER—TRUE POWER!	**113**
Daily Reflection	116

28. THE POWER OF JESUS' NAME — 117
   Daily Reflection — 119

29. JESUS' PRAYER AND PLEA — 121
   Daily Reflection — 123

30. LABORING FOR SOULS — 125
   Daily Reflection — 128

31. THE AMEN — 129
   Jesus Is God's Amen — 130
   Jesus Is Amen in Himself — 131
   Jesus Is God's Amen to Every Christian — 132
   Daily Reflection — 132

About C. H. Spurgeon — 135
References — 137

© Copyright 2022 by GodliPress. All rights reserved.

This book is copyright protected. It is only for personal use. You cannot amend, distribute, sell, use, quote or paraphrase any part, or the content within this book, without the consent of the author or publisher, except in the case of brief quotations embodied in critical articles or reviews.

Scripture quotations are from The ESV® Bible (The Holy Bible, English Standard Version®), copyright © 2001 by Crossway, a publishing ministry of Good News Publishers. Used by permission. All rights reserved.

INTRODUCTION

The name Spurgeon carries incredible weight, even after more than 100 years. It is a testament to the respect and admiration Christians across denominations have for his insight and ability to convey spiritual matters simply and clearly.

His rich words and simple approach remain a treasure for pastors, theologians, and ordinary Christians looking to grow and expand their walk with the Lord. It is no wonder then, that every effort has been made to preserve and make his sermons, books, and teachings available across different formats. Institutions, centers, and websites exist for the sole purpose of bringing these gems to the public.

Apart from having a special consideration for the lost, prayer was one of Spurgeon's favorite topics. As part of the 'Prayersify' series that promotes and encourages personal and corporate prayer, it was important to include his thoughts and revelations on the topic.

Arranging Spurgeon's ideas and perceptions on the topic of prayer was no easy task. Choosing from 3,500 of his different sermons took time, careful consideration, and prayer. Added to that, much work went into condensing the lectures into bite-sized daily readings, as well as making it palatable for our modern English readers.

As a result of abridging his words to fit into the layout of this book, many of Spurgeon's stories that he is so well known for had to be left out, along with other perceptive nuggets. To gain the full beauty and impact, it will be worth your while to get hold of the specific sermons in their entirety from one of the many websites that honor his legacy.

The aim in this 31-day approach is to bring these timeless gems into an easy-to-handle format without losing the effect of the original. Setting aside a month and focusing on the different aspects each day, each reading will be a challenge and inspiration for your prayer life. To give even more room for Spurgeon's words to have an impact, study questions have been added to allow for deeper reflection. Allow the Holy Spirit to guide you as you work through these and contemplate their meaning for your own life.

Our desire is that prayer will become deep, special, and powerful to you. As Spurgeon said, "I would rather teach **one** man to pray than **ten** men to preach."

1

A CALL TO PRAYER

"On your walls, O Jerusalem, I have set watchmen; all the day and all the night they shall never be silent. You who put the LORD in remembrance, take no rest, and give him no rest until he establishes Jerusalem and makes it a praise in the earth"
Isaiah 62:6-7

A Call

We are called to be **watchmen**. In times of war, every fortified city had them on its walls. Whoever passed that way was challenged, and if he was an enemy, the watchmen sounded an alarm for the city to be protected against attack. God's people should act as watchmen on the walls. In the Roman days, a sentry never thought of quitting his post. Christians are put in their positions, and they must stand strong, because they have received their commands from the King Himself.

We do not just guard by day only, but during the darkest night we are to maintain our watch. *"All the day and all the night."* We are never off duty. Ours is a life service, and a constant service. Our service of the Lord's cause is not just on Sundays but as often as we have opportunity.

But, in the next place, we are to be **spokesmen**, always ready to speak a word in season. *"They shall never be silent."* By prayer you unlock the treasuries of heaven—keep the key constantly turning. As speakers heavenward and earthward, never hold your peace day nor night.

We are also called to be **record keepers** or those that remind—*"You who put the LORD in remembrance, take no rest."* Kings had an officer to remind them of the promises they had made. The Lord has appointed His praying people to be His record keepers. God cannot forget, but He calls us to act as if He could, and put Him in remembrance. By reminding the Lord of His promises, we become better acquainted with them. If we pray without a promise, we have no reason to expect an answer.

A Caution

"Take no rest." Always be praying. If not always in the act of prayer, always be in the spirit of prayer. *"Pray without ceasing"* (1 Thess. 5:17). Do not just reason with Him, but wrestle with God in prayer. Sometimes pray without words, and sometimes with them. Pray alone, and pray often with others.

"*Watch and pray*" (Matt. 26:41)—that sums up our verse. Never rest from prayer because you are tired of it. Whenever prayer becomes unpleasant, it should be a loud warning to pray even more. When a person gets tired of breathing, then they must be dying; when a person gets tired of praying, we should be worried about them, because they are in a bad way.

Never rest from prayer because you have prayed enough. When has anyone prayed enough? I have heard of soldiers sleeping while on the march, and I have known some good people sleep while praying, till I have thought that their prayers were a kind of pious snore.

Above all, let us never rest out of despair.

A Command

"*Give him no rest.*" Give God no rest! I am amazed at such a command. I am sure none of you ever told a beggar to be persistent with you. Persistence is commanded, is influential, with God. Jesus reminds us of this in His parables! The widow who seeks justice from a judge. Her perseverance is a model and an encouragement for us. Another man has a friend who arrives at his door in the night asking for bread. We should persist like this until God's door is opened! You may have what you will if you understand the art of persistence. It would not have been commanded had it not been right for us, and prevalent with God. God is moved by the persistent prayers of His people.

Take no rest from prayer, and give Him no rest.

Daily Reflection

These daily reflections are an addition. Instead of taking the place of the reading or adding any significant revelations, they are meant to guide you to think more about what has just been read, about how it relates to your own life, and about what you might need to change.

1. Do you see yourself as a watchman, spokesman, or record keeper? Why?
2. What is your first reaction to the words, "*All the day and all the night*"? What do you understand by them?
3. Read Matthew 26:36-46. How do you relate to the disciples and their response to the command, "*Watch and pray*"?
4. What is the difference between being in the "act of prayer" and the "spirit of prayer"?
5. Are you persistent in prayer? Do you find it easy?

2

ENCOURAGEMENT TO PRAY

"I am the LORD your God, who brought you up out of the land of Egypt. Open your mouth wide, and I will fill it"
Psalm 81:10

The verse before this one tells us to turn away from any strange God: *"There shall be no strange god among you; you shall not bow down to a foreign god"* (Psalm 81:9). Idolatry is not just bowing before idols; the essence of it lies in putting trust in anything other than God. We can easily make gods of our experience, wealth, talents, children, wives, husbands, friends, and anything by valuing it more than our Savior.

In our verse, God comes near to His people and encourages them to come nearer to Him. He opens His mouth to them, that they may open their mouths to Him.

Encouragement

God encourages us by saying, *"Open your mouth wide"* to help us to **get rid of any fear**. Do you feel as if you cannot pray? You might be afraid to come before the Lord, you dare not take hold of the horns of the altar, you think that it would be too bold to look to Jesus for mercy. But the Father says, *"Open your mouth!* Speak, my child; my ear is waiting to hear your cry."

Next, *"Open your mouth wide"* means **being able to speak freely in prayer** to God. We want freedom to come to God. You are not before a judge, enemy, or someone who will criticize you; the Lord is love and gentleness to those who seek His face. What have you done? What do you want? Open your mouth wide, let it all come out, hide nothing from God.

The phrase also means **asking for and expecting great things**. Usually, the smaller the favor, the more likely you are to obtain it, but with God it is the other way—the greater the gift you ask for, the more sure you are to have it. There is nothing greater to ask for than Jesus. If you ask for wealth, you may not get it, for it is a small thing which the Lord might not care to give you, but if you ask for eternal life, you will have it, for this is a great thing, and God delights to give the greatest blessings to those who come to Him in Jesus.

The less you expect from man, the better, but the more you expect from God, the more you are likely to receive. I think this encouragement means we should have a great expectancy. Have you ever seen little birds inside a nest when they expected their mother to feed them? She seems to say, *"Open your mouth wide, and I will fill it."*

Reasons

The first reason why you should open your mouth wide is **because of what God has done**. He says, *"I am the LORD your God, who brought you up out of the land of Egypt."*

God has done just that same kind of thing for all His people. We are no longer under the power of sin and Satan, the Lord has set us free. If this does not lead us to open our mouths wide in prayer, what will? God says to you that He has brought His people out of Egypt, and He who has done that can do anything.

The second reason is **because of what God will do**—*"Open your mouth wide, and I will fill it."*

There is a story that the Shah of Persia said to a person who had pleased him, *"Open your mouth wide."* When the man opened his mouth, the Shah began to fill it up with diamonds, emeralds, rubies, and all sorts of precious stones. I am sure that the man opened his mouth wide, he made it as large as it could go, whether it looked beautiful or not. Wouldn't you do the same if you had such an opportunity?

The Lord says to His own people, whom He favors, *"Open your mouth wide, and I will fill it."* God gives prayer as well as the answer to prayer. God loves to look for emptiness where He can store His grace.

Daily Reflection

We always need encouragement to keep going, to do better, to not give up. It can be at work, in our family life, and even in our spiritual aspirations. Wherever we are in life, we all need constant motivation to make sure we will finish the race strong. Here, Spurgeon shows us the encouragement to pray from God Himself.

1. There is a brief look at Psalm 81:9, but what connection does it have with verse 10?
2. What do you understand about "opening your mouth wide" in relation to your prayer life?
3. Expect less from man, but more from God. Do you agree with this?
4. Why is knowing what God has done and what He will do important to prayer?
5. What is the 'emptiness' that God loves to fill?

3

WHEN SHOULD WE PRAY?

"They ought always to pray and not lose heart"
Luke 18:1

Look at the first word of the verse, *"**They** ought always to pray."* I am so happy it does not say, "Saints ought always to pray," because then I would ask if I were a saint or not. Who should always pray, then? *"They."* And that is generic and includes men, women, children—all who are human should pray. The word *'ought'* implies permission. If you have a head on your shoulders, and lungs that breathe, and a heart that beats, this verse is for you.

Now, let us put the emphasis on another word. *"They ought **always** to pray."* *'Always'* includes this present moment. So, you can pray now. "Well, I will rush home and pray." Do not do that. Sit down where you are and let your soul breathe out to God. "But I would like to get down on my knees." Yes, but there is no need for it. Get on the knees of your soul.

Let me try and open this up a little. *"They ought always to pray"* means praying in all circumstances. Whatever the difficulty or the issue is, pray about it. If it is a domestic issue, a business matter, or a church problem—pray about it. My advice is to "Take it to the Lord in prayer." Whatever the difficulty is, whatever shape it takes, secular or religious, *"They ought always to pray,"*—they should pray about everything. This is the remedy that will cure all diseases. This is the key that fits every lock in the prison-house of our sorrow.

"They ought always to pray." We should always pray because we always have sin to confess, something to thank God for, and needs to be supplied. If you are down in the valley, you need prayer to be able to climb the hill. If you are on the hill, you need to pray twice as much that you do not grow dizzy and fall down. If you do not have, pray until you have. If your cup is empty, pray for the Lord to fill it. If your cup is full, pray for God to make your hand steady that you do not spill. If you cannot see your way, pray for God to guide you. If you can see your way, pray for God to help you follow it.

Are you young? Pray for God to help you against the sins of youth. Are you in the middle of life? Pray for God to help you in the middle passage, where trials are many. Are you almost into heaven with age? Pray that you may enter heaven with prayer.

"Pray without ceasing" (1 Thess 5:17) is a clear, clean-cut command. There is no getting over that verse. *"They ought*

always to pray," or else we take the matter out of God's hands—we always need God's help, whether we think we do or not.

The intention of this verse is not just to teach continuity in prayer but rather persistence in prayer. It does not mean always praying but rather to keep on praying for a specific thing. You are to continue to pray. You do not have to stop work or domestic chores to pray. You can do those and pray at the same time, and this is how Christians should always pray.

Then we should pray even if there has been a long delay in answers to our prayers. Persevere in the prayer with this verse to encourage you, *"They ought always to pray."* If it is something that only concerns your own personal comfort, then God's Spirit may teach you to limit your prayers. *"Three times I pleaded with the Lord about this,"* said Paul, *"that it should leave me"* (2 Cor. 12:8). He did not get the answer he wanted, but he was given one that satisfied him. God did not take away the thorn in the flesh, but He said, *"My grace is sufficient for you"* (2 Cor 12:9). Paul still had to bear the trial, but he received grace from the Lord to help him bear it.

"They ought always to pray and not lose heart." If you do not pray, you will get tired and faint. There are some who faint fatally. A religion that does not begin with secret prayer is not worth the label you put on it! A religion that is not sustained by secret prayer is a lie. A religion that does not grow through secret prayer may be puffed up, but it is not truly built up by the hand of God.

Wait on Him for fresh strength and then you will come out as though you washed your face in the dew of heaven, the light of God entered your eyes, and you will come with new words as the Spirit gives. *"Wait for the Lord,"* (Isa. 40:31) because this is what will keep you from fainting and help you to renew your strength like the eagle's.

Daily Reflection

'Always' is a word we use so often that it loses its significance. We argue with it in sweeping terms, and love to scatter it in between complaints. In the context of this reading, it seems a tall order, a harsh requirement, and a bit extreme. Yet, no matter which translation of the Bible we use, it is still the same.

1. Read this verse in other versions of the Bible. What is meant by the word 'ought'?
2. Answer these questions in your own understanding:
3. Why should we always pray?
4. How should we always pray?
5. When should we always pray?
6. Do you find it easy to always pray?
7. What is the connection between always praying and not losing heart?

4

MY HOURLY PRAYER

"Hold me up, that I may be safe and have regard for your statutes continually!"
Psalm 119:117

The verse before this says, *"Uphold me"* (Psalm 119:116). They are two notes from the same bell, teaching us the importance of the prayer. This prayer shows David's need to be upheld, a strong conviction that God could uphold Him, and an expectation and hope that He would surely do so in answer to his prayer.

The Need

A Christian is someone who walks in uprightness, but the danger is that they might not continue upright.

They cannot walk upright unless they are upheld, for **the way is slippery**. I have noticed that more people sin without temptation than with it, and that the worst falls occur on level roads where there seems to be no stone to trip them up.

We also have **weak knees**, and hands that hang down. The most we can do is just to stand leaning on Jesus, but to stand upright on a rough road is more than we can handle. So, we need to pray, *"Hold me up."*

But that is not all, for there are **cunning enemies** that want to trip us up. They lay traps for us. Some threaten, others flatter. A few would bribe us, more would bully us. There is only One who can guide you safely, but if you do not follow Him, you will slip. Therefore, we have a reason to say, *"Hold me up."*

How does God keep His people upright? He can preserve you by angels; *"they will bear you up, lest you strike your foot against a stone"* (Psalm 91:12). At other times God holds up His people by the ministry of the word. Wherever it is faithfully spoken, it is a wall of fire round about God's people. Often, God keeps His people upright, and holds them firmly, by discipline. *"Before I was afflicted I went astray, but now I keep your word"* (Psalm 119:67). God can hold us up by these and many other methods.

The Result

If God upholds us, then, according to the verse, we will *"be safe."* You will be safe from all real harm. Suppose you have trouble in business, you will still be safe if God upholds you, so that you do not lose your integrity. The person that damages their character has sustained the worst damage anyone can know, but the person that is held up—kept upright—has been kept safely. They may be slandered, but if they know that before God they have walked uprightly, they will *"be safe."* You will also be safe from falling into dangerous sin. If God keeps you from evil, how happy you are, because you are *'safe'*!

When we know that we are *'safe'* by God's grace, then we will also *"have regard for your statutes continually."* Being alert and attentive goes with safety, and is its fruit and its sign. A holy person has great respect for every command of God. Unless we respect all the commandments, we will soon be sinning and getting into danger.

Every morning before you see people, pray, *"Hold me up, that I may be safe and have regard for your statutes continually!"* Are you going downstairs without that prayer? Then you may sin at the breakfast table, maybe lose your temper. Therefore, pray before the car moves. You are going off to work, are you tempted there? Then breathe the prayer, *"Hold me up, that I may be safe."*

Do not be nervous, but be prayerful. Ask the Lord to help you. Ask Him to help you about everything.

Young people, you must pray, for your passions are strong, and your wisdom is little. Those who are old, do not stop asking for upholding grace. The worst falls I have ever seen in the church have happened to elderly people with lots of experience.

"Now to him who is able to keep you from stumbling and to present you blameless before the presence of his glory with great joy, to the only God, our Savior, through Jesus Christ our Lord, be glory, majesty, dominion, and authority, before all time and now and forever. Amen" (Jude 1:24-25).

Daily Reflection

The title of this reading is the original one Spurgeon used for his sermon over 100 years ago. But it is still significant for us today to know that we should be praying throughout the day, asking the Lord to sustain us and "hold us up." Have your Bible close by as you read these chapters and work through the daily reflection questions. Look up any related verses, and use the cross-reference if you have it.

1. Which of the needs that are listed do you often find you need to pray to be upheld for?
2. How does God uphold you? Can you think of actual examples?
3. Do you ever feel safe, the way the word is used by Spurgeon? If not, why?
4. What connection does obeying commandments have here?

5

PERSONAL COMMUNION

"Give ear, O Lord, to my prayer; listen to my plea for grace. In the day of my trouble I call upon you, for you answer me."
Psalm 86:6-7

There are two things which David must have when he prays—two great things after which he strains with his whole heart. The first is personal communion with God. Read that sixth verse, *"Give ear, O Lord, to my prayer; listen to my plea for grace."*

Note that David, while he wanted to come to close grips with the Lord in prayer, was not arrogant. He understands that fellowship means God coming down to us. We can see this in his first line, *"Incline your ear, O Lord, and answer me"* (Psalm 86:1). This is what we must have for true prayer. Our prayer must climb to that great ear. Isn't there something wonderful about this, that we, who are both insignificant and unworthy, should be able to speak to Him who made the stars, and upholds all things by the word of His power?

This is the essence of prayer; in human weakness to talk with omnipotence, in nothingness to deal with all-sufficiency. You cannot do this without the Mediator, Jesus. With the Mediator, what a wonderful fellowship we are allowed to enjoy with the infinite God!

As we read further in this psalm, we will notice that David, in order to obtain this privilege, pleads his need for it. He cries, *"I am poor and needy"* (Psalm 86:1). You cannot say to God, "Lord, look at me, and commune with me, for I am somebody." God will not condescend to your pride, He will turn His back upon you, but if you come to Him with a beggar's claim—an appeal to the charity of God's sovereign love, then He will turn and hear your prayer.

In order to come into communion with God, David pleads his personal consecration, *"Preserve my life, for I am godly"* (Psalm 86:2). By this I understand that he belongs to God, that he is consecrated and dedicated to Him. David, anxious to use every argument, also pleads his trust, *"Save your servant, who trusts in you"* (Psalm 86:2). You may expect to find God drawing near to you, if you are holding to Him as your confidence. David urges yet another reason why he should see God, because he is always in prayer, *"to you do I cry all the day"* (Psalm 86:3).

David also tells the Lord that he could not get as close to God as he wanted to, but he struggled and strained to do so.

Is this not the meaning of the expression, *"Gladden the soul of your servant, for to you, O Lord, do I lift up my soul"* (Psalm 86:4)? We should either be rejoicing in the Lord or longing after Him! Ask God to make you miserable, unless His conscious presence makes you happy.

David, conscious of the great privilege he wanted and asked for, was not content without pleading the greatest argument of all, he pleads the goodness of the Lord. Read it in verse five, *"For you, O Lord, are good."* As much as to say—If You were not good You would never listen to me. But, there is sin in us. For the holy God not to be kept back by our sinfulness, this is a great mystery. But then the verse says He is *"good and forgiving."*

In prayer, it is vital for us to really speak with God. If we just repeat good words, what is the use of it? You might as well stand on a hill and talk to the moon as kneel down and hurry through the Lord's Prayer, and then think that you have prayed. I tell you, you might better do the first than the second, for you would not insult God in that case, whereas you do insult Him in every one of those holy words which you use without thought, heart, and faith.

If your prayer does not come from your heart, it will not go to God's heart, and if it does not bring you near to God so that you are speaking to Him, you have simply wasted your breath.

Daily Reflection

This reading highlights the close relationship that David had with God, and the close relationship we can enjoy in prayer. Communion is often just used to describe the Lord's Supper, but its deeper meaning is to share or exchange intimate thoughts and feelings on a spiritual level. When we see how integral prayer is, we can appreciate David's words even more.

1. Read the whole of Psalm 86. See it in the light of an intimate, personal conversation with God.
2. Do you ever pray in a manner similar to this, "to really speak with God"?
3. Do you sometimes think God does not "incline His ear" to you? Why?
4. How many arguments does David use in this prayer? Do you use any in your prayers?

6

PERSONAL ANSWERS

"Give ear, O Lord, to my prayer; listen to my plea for grace. In the day of my trouble I call upon you, for you answer me."
Psalm 86:6-7

The second thing David must have when he prays—personal answers from God. He is not content to pray without prayer having some practical result. So, the next verse is, *"In the day of my trouble I call upon you, for you answer me."*

When we pray, we expect God to hear us. I like the remark of an old lady, who, when her prayer was answered, was asked, "Does it not surprise you?" She said, "No, it does not surprise me, it is just like Him." A prayer should be the presentation of God's promise endorsed by your personal faith.

Some people pray for an hour together. I am happy that they can, but I cannot always do this, and I see no need for it. It is like a person going into a bank with a check and waiting for an hour. The sensible thing is to go to the counter, show your check, take your money, and go about your business. Sometimes a flood of words only means excusing unbelief. As a general rule, faith presents its prayer, gets its answer, and goes on its way rejoicing.

We expect our God to answer our prayer even more when we are in trouble. David expected the same; *"In the day of my trouble I call upon you, for you answer me."* Trouble is sent to make us pray. When we pray, the prayer becomes the relief for our trouble, and when the prayer is heard, it becomes the salvation out of our trouble. Many of us would be out of trouble quickly if we prayed. Often trial has to rap our fingers to make us let go of our harmful confidences and turn to the Lord. With our vain-confidence, we are like a madman with a razor; the more we grasp it, the more it cuts us. Drop the deadly self-trust; trust in God, and look to Him, and your deliverance will quickly come to you.

Now, if we expect God to answer us, we have grounds to believe it. I have a right to believe that God will hear prayer, otherwise why is prayer commanded? The Bible is full of prayer. If there is no God that hears prayer, I shall not pray, nor will any other rational person. Prayer gives us the assurance that God intends to hear and to answer. There have been believers of different molds and characters, but they have all prayed.

Why does the throne of grace still remain as a permanent institution, of which Paul says, *"Let us then with confidence draw near to the throne of grace"* (Heb. 4:16), unless there is a reality in it? Why is Jesus the way to the mercy seat? Why is He the Intercessor and Mediator, if there is nothing in prayer? What is the Holy Spirit doing by helping us to present petitions that will never reach the ear of God?

I declare that no fact is better proved by my experience than this, that the Lord hears the prayers of His believing people. You will know for yourselves whether there is a God that hears prayer. Does He answer your requests?

You may say, "There are so many problems with prayer being heard." Are there? There are problems with eating, breathing, sleeping, and the air filled with disease, and yet we are still alive. The difficulties connected with prayer are philosophical difficulties, not practical ones. If you are philosophers, you spend all your time wondering about them, but if you are simple, practical people, you pray and receive the blessing. What if you stop wondering, and just do as God tells you, and see whether it does not work.

I cannot expect anyone to believe that they can commune with God, or that God will hear their prayer, and grant their desire, unless they have personally been led to try it. That person has entered a new life, capable of understanding new things. When we are born again, then our inner life turns to the life of God, and has fellowship with Him and He answers.

You must draw nearer, and nearer, or love will not rest. As when one comes into the sunshine, he feels the warmth, so when we come nearer to God we have more joy in Him. Keep near to God, grow in prayer, let your supplications be instant and constant, and you will be sure that the Father Himself hears your cries!

Daily Reflection

Following on from the reading before this one, we find that David pleads because he believes he will be answered. This faith and confidence as we pray is important but not always easy to have. Believing in what we are speaking to the Lord about is critical to the effectiveness of our prayers.

1. What do you think the link between communion and answers is?
2. Spurgeon gives us the picture of waiting in a bank or simply walking straight in and cashing the check. When it comes to prayer, which one describes you more?
3. Look at Hebrews 4:16. What is the difference between arrogance and confidence?
4. Why do we have a right to believe God will answer us?
5. Are you more practical or philosophical? Does this help or hinder your prayers?

7

LEAD US NOT INTO TEMPTATION

"And lead us not into temptation, but deliver us from evil"
Matthew 6:13

The Lord's Prayer could be called a Prayer of Degrees. It begins with the spirit of adoption, *"Our Father"* (Matt. 6:9). There is no acceptable prayer until we can say the words of the prodigal son—*"I will arise and go to my father"* (Luke 15:18). This child-like spirit sees the glory of the Father *"in heaven,"* and goes on to adoration, *"hallowed be your name."* The child who says, *"Abba! Father!"* (Gal. 4:6), grows into the angel that cries out, *"Holy, holy, holy"* (Rev. 4:8).

There is only one step from worship to the missionary spirit —*"Your kingdom come, your will be done, on earth as it is in heaven"* (Matt. 6:10). We do not start our spiritual journey with this mission spirit, we begin with *"Our Father."* We go on to feel His glory, and the next natural desire is that others may also know His greatness, until we are ready to cry, *"May the whole earth be filled with his glory!"* (Psalm 72:19).

In the process of education, which this prayer describes so well, we are first conscious of our dependence on God, because we say, *"Give us this day our daily bread"* (Matt. 6:11). Becoming enlightened by the Spirit, we discover that we are not just dependent but sinful, so we beg for mercy—*"Forgive us our debts, as we also have forgiven our debtors"* (Matt. 6:12), and being forgiven, having the righteousness of Christ, and knowing God accepts us, we humbly pray for perseverance—*"Lead us not into temptation."* If we are really forgiven, we do not want to offend again, justification leads to a desire for sanctification. *"Forgive us our debts"* is justification, *"Lead us not into temptation, but deliver us from evil"* is sanctification.

Many people are confused by the verse that says, *"Let no one say when he is tempted, 'I am being tempted by God,' for God cannot be tempted with evil, and he himself tempts no one"* (James 1:13). It is difficult to reconcile this statement with the Lord's Prayer, and people have even altered Jesus' words to fit. The Greek does not say, "Leave us not in temptation," but *"Lead us not into temptation."*

The word temptation has two meanings: to test, and to entice. When we read that God tempted Abraham, we should not understand that He enticed Abraham to anything that was evil; the meaning of the word in that place is simply and only that God tested him, but this interpretation does not fit with our key verse. The word used for 'temptation' is not the word constantly written for a test or trial. It is the word we use if temptation to sin is meant.

You might ask, "If God does not tempt men, how can we pray, 'Lead us not into temptation'"? The verse does not say, "Do not tempt us," but it says, "*Lead us not into temptation,*" and we will see there is a huge difference between leading into temptation and actually tempting. God tempts no one. For God to tempt us by enticing us to sin is inconsistent with His nature and character, but for God to lead us into those conflicts with evil which we call temptations is not only possible but common.

Often, the Great Captain of Salvation leads us into battle where we must face evil and conquer through the blood of the Lamb, and this leading into temptation is by divine grace for our good, since by being tempted we grow strong in grace and patience. Our God and Father may lead us into places where Satan, the world, and the flesh may tempt us, and the prayer is to be understood in that sense.

God never leads men into temptation so that He is to blame for their sin if they fall into it. God cannot possibly become a conspirator with us in our crimes. John Trapp said, "God tempts men for **probation**, but never for **perdition**." The devil tempts us that he can ruin us; God tests us, and puts them where Satan may try us, but He does it for probation, that the chaff may be sifted from the wheat, that the impurities may be separated from the fine gold. In these trials, hypocrites fall. It is like a rough wind that sweeps through the forest and snaps the rotten branch from the tree. The fault is not in the wind but in the rotten branch.

While the benefits that God brings out of us being led into temptation are great, temptation in itself is so dangerous, trials and distress are so perilous, that it is right for the Christian to pray, *"Lead us not into temptation."* Martin Luther says, "Temptation is the best school into which the Christian can enter, yet, in itself, apart from the grace of God, it is so hazardous, that this prayer should be offered every day, 'Lead us not into temptation,' or if we must enter into it, 'Lord, deliver us from evil.'"

Daily Reflection

The Lord's Prayer is often recited, sung, or revered without really understanding the words. Spurgeon's ability to unpack and teach us the context and spiritual essence of this timeless piece is startling and challenging. Putting the format aside and looking at it with new eyes can bring a revelation of what Jesus was trying to show his disciples, and us.

1. A helpful exercise would be to write out the Lord's Prayer and list the 'steps' or 'degrees' as Spurgeon sees them. Matthew 6:9-13.
2. Why do you think Jesus saw it as important to start with the "spirit of adoption"?
3. Spurgeon takes his time to explain temptation. Why is this important to understand in this context?
4. How does James 1:13-15 emphasize this?
5. What is the difference between probation and perdition?
6. Do you ever pray the Lord's Prayer? Why?

8

LET US PRAY

"But for me it is good to be near God"
Psalm 73:28

There are many ways Christians draw near to God, but prayer is the best.

To help, we will look at the verse as a touchstone, where we can measure and gauge our prayers. Then we will see it as a grindstone to sharpen our desires, to make us more sincere, and more diligent in prayer, because *"it is good to be near God."* Lastly, I will use it as a tombstone, with an inscription for those who do not know what it is to draw near to God, for "A prayerless soul is a Christless soul."

A Touchstone

It cannot be prayer if we do not draw near to God.

If you use a format of prayer, have you drawn near to God while you have been repeating those words? If not, you have said prayers, but you have never prayed in your life.

Maybe you have been repeating prayers, and have ignorantly imagined that you have prayed. Your prayer has never been presented. You have not brought it before the bleeding Lamb of God, and have not asked Him to take it for you into the sacred place, and present the request with His own merits before His Father's throne.

On the other hand, you might offer a spontaneous prayer—have you drawn near to God? You have offered sacrifice, but it has been on your own high places, and the sacrifice has been an abomination. You have not brought it to God's altar, you have not come up to the mercy seat, where He is present! You have not drawn near to God, and consequently, your prayers, though there are many of them, are utterly useless to your soul's benefit. Drawing near to God is an indispensable requisite in accepted prayer.

You must draw near to God in at least one of three levels: either in a lowly sense of His majesty, in a delightful consciousness of his goodness, or a ravishing sense of your own relationship to Him. Otherwise, your prayer is worthless—whispering to the wind, a cry to the desert air, where no one can hear or help you. Bring your prayers to this touchstone and let God examine them, and be honest with yourselves, for your own soul's sake.

A Grindstone

The first thing that will sharpen our desires in prayer is this—**prayer explains mysteries**. Asaph in Psalm 73 had been greatly troubled trying to understand how God could be just and give riches to the wicked while His own people were in poverty. At last, he understood it all because he went into the house of God. And he says—looking back on his discovery—*"But for me it is good to be near God."* If you learn something on your knees, you will never unlearn it. What people can teach you, they can unteach you. But if God has taught them to me, I have learned that I shall never unlearn, nor forget.

A second grindstone for your prayers shall be this—**prayer brings deliverance**. If we would have deliverance in the hour, "Let us pray." Prayer will soon bring merciful deliverance from the throne of our faithful God. God has given each one of His people the promise: "As often as you are in need or sorrow, show it to Me, and I will deliver you."

The third is—**prayer obtains promises.** Prayer clears the sky. Prayer is a heaven climber. Prayer even makes Satan tremble. But make sure it is real prayer, because if it is not, and the promise is not brought to God's attention, you may never obtain the blessing. Draw near to God with living, loving prayer, present the promise, and you will receive what you are after.

There is a fourth reason to be diligent in prayer—**it has the power to sustain the soul in every season of despair and sorrow**. Whenever the heart becomes weak, use the heavenly strengthening plaster of prayer. It was in prayer that the angel appeared to Jesus and strengthened Him. That angel has appeared to many of us, and we have not forgotten the strength we received when we were on our knees.

A Tombstone

Christianity is more serious work than many of us think.

I am often shocked at the superficial way in which people spend all their time. If you only knew what you are made for and your destiny, you would not waste your time on the insignificant things that occupy your hands and your hearts. God forgive the wasted hours that Christians should be busy using for the good of others. God forgive those moments that should have been occupied in prayer.

Maybe you have never prayed in your life. If you have never looked for and never found the Savior, if you have never seen the scars of Jesus, if you have never looked to Him, your eyes will not just be closed in death, but they will see a terrible eternity. May God give you the grace to pray, to fall on your knees, and for the first time to cry, "Lord have mercy on me!"

Daily Reflection

Spurgeon often used a clever three-point sermon approach when preaching, and this is very obvious in this reading. It helps us to remember the points, and then recall the teaching attached to those. By using three different types of stone, he highlights the importance of prayer for us.

1. A touchstone was used to identify the purity of metals. Why is this a perfect heading for section 1?
2. What are the three levels that Spurgeon says we should draw near to God?
3. What are the four things that will sharpen our desire in prayer? Which one is easiest for you to understand? Which is the hardest?
4. Why is a tombstone used?

9

THANKSGIVING TO THE FATHER

> *"Giving thanks to the Father, who has qualified you to share in the inheritance of the saints in light. He has delivered us from the domain of darkness and transferred us to the kingdom of his beloved Son"*
> Colossians 1:12-13

We are told to give *"thanks to the Father."* We do not always need to be told to give thanks to the Son—his body hanging on the cross is always present in our faith. It is the same with the Holy Spirit. We feel our dependence on His constant influence every day. If there is one Person in the Trinity whom we often forget, it is God the Father.

The Spirit comes from God the Father, and whatever acts are performed by the Spirit are actually done by the Father, because he sends the Spirit. The works of the Son of God are all linked with the Father. If the Son came into the world, it is because the Father sent him; if the Son calls his people, it is because his Father gave them into his hands.

If we look at the verse, we will see the reason for giving thanks to the Father, because of the blessings he has given us.

The first blessing is that the Father *"has qualified you to share in the inheritance of the saints in light."* It is a present blessing, to share in the inheritance at this very moment. What does this mean? Does it mean that the believer is perfect; that he is free from sin? No, it means we are accepted in the Beloved, adopted into the family. The Greek word for *qualified* is 'suitable' or 'sufficient.' He has made us sufficient *"to share in the inheritance of the saints in light."*

We do not need a new thing to be implanted, but God has already put it there when we were born again, and it will be made to grow until it comes to perfection and we enter into *"the inheritance of the saints in light."*

So, are we already made ready and sufficient for the inheritance of heaven? Who qualifies for an inheritance? Sons. Who makes us sons? *"Behold, what manner of love the Father hath bestowed upon us, that we should be called the sons of God"* (1 John 3:1 KJV). The moment the son is born, he is an heir. All that is needed is that he grows up and is capable of possession. Just being a son, he qualifies for an inheritance. It is the Father's choice to adopt us into his family and qualify us for inheritance.

This makes us grateful to the Father.

The second blessing looks back on the gloomy past, and the dangers from which we have escaped. *"He has delivered us from the domain of darkness."* We were under the power of darkness. All of us were under this power once, but the Father *"has delivered us from the domain of darkness and transferred us to the kingdom of his beloved Son."*

Now, look at the connection between the two verses. Verse 12 tells me that the inheritance of heaven is the inheritance of light. Then I can see my qualification for it described in verse 13—He delivered me from the power of darkness. Is that not the same thing? If I am delivered from the power of darkness, is that not being made sufficient to live in the light? I do not only have the light spoken of in verse 12 but the sonship, too, because I am in *"the kingdom of his beloved Son."*

When we are brought into the kingdom of God's Son, we are made sons. It is an inheritance; and when we are brought into the inherited kingdom of God's dear Son, we enjoy the inheritance now, and are qualified to enjoy it forever.

This is the Father's work. Shouldn't we love God the Father, give Him thanks, sing to Him, and exalt His name?

Daily Reflection

Thanksgiving is a large part of prayer, often overlooked or rushed through in order to get through our long list of requests. But, even when we are grateful, we often focus on Jesus and forget to express our gratitude to the Father. Spurgeon highlights the importance of seeing the role He plays in our lives and thanking Him for it.

1. Why is the Father so important? What role does he play in the Trinity?
2. What are the two blessings talked about in this reading?
3. Spurgeon shows that verses 12 and 13 are interconnected. Can you explain their relationship?
4. Do you ever thank the Father?
5. Look at these verses: Matthew 11:25, Luke 10:21, Ephesians 1:3, 5:18-20.

10

PRAYING IN THE HOLY SPIRIT

"Praying in the Holy Spirit"
Jude 1:20

See the order of the verse in context. The righteous are described as first *"building yourselves up in your most holy faith"* (Jude 1:20). What then follows faith? Is it not prayer, *"Praying in the Holy Spirit"*? The person who has no faith has no prayer. See what follows after that: *"Keep yourselves in the love of God"* (Jude 1:21). Prayer builds an altar and lays the sacrifice and the wood in order, and then love, like the priest, brings holy fire from heaven and sets the offering in a blaze. Faith is the root of grace, prayer is the stalk, and love is the flower.

However, there is a step beyond love. It is believing expectantly, *"waiting for the mercy of our Lord Jesus Christ that leads to eternal life"* (Jude 1:21). Hope climbs the staircase that faith has built, and bowing on the knees of prayer, looks through the window love has opened, and sees Jesus coming in His glory with eternal life for His people.

While there are many different types of prayers, they are only acceptable to God if they are *"in the Holy Spirit."* The prayer that is not in the Holy Spirit is in the flesh, those who are in the flesh cannot please God. Only the prayer which comes from God can go to God. The desire He writes on our heart will move His heart and bring a blessing, but the desires of the flesh have no power with Him.

Let us look at this verse as a test, tonic, and map for our prayers.

A Test

Examine yourselves carefully. Have you prayed in the Holy Spirit? Has He made you feel it in your heart? Doesn't God hate the sacrifice that has no heart? The body may be on its knees, but the heart is far from the mercy seat. The only prayer acceptable to God is a heart-prayer, a soul-prayer, and a prayer which the Holy Spirit moves us to pray. Everything else is beating the air and being busy in vain.

Come, and lay your prayers on this threshing floor, and thresh them with this verse, *"Praying in the Holy Spirit."* How much straw and excess rubbish there will be, and how little actual, real grain!

A Tonic

I understand that *"Praying in the Holy Spirit"* means that the Holy Spirit is willing to help me to pray, that He will tell me how to pray, and that when I get to a point where I cannot express my desires, He will make intercession in me with groans which cannot be uttered. Jesus, in His agony, was strengthened by an angel, you are to be supported by God Himself. Aaron and Hur held up the hands of Moses, but the Holy Spirit Himself helps your weaknesses. God does not want words. He never reads our petitions according to our outward words, but according to the inner groaning. Remember that the outside of prayer is just a shell, the inside of prayer is its true essence.

A Map

What does praying in the Holy Spirit mean? The words can be translated, "by the Holy Spirit," or "through the Holy Spirit," as well as, "in the Holy Spirit," and means praying in the Holy Spirit's power. The natural mind knows nothing about this. We know that the Spirit, without the use of sounds, speaks in our hearts; without words, the ear can hear, He can make our soul know His presence and understand His meaning. Our spirit prays because it is overshadowed and filled with the power of the Holy Spirit.

We should wait on God in prayer, asking Him to reveal those matters we should plead with Him? Beware of hit-or-miss prayers. Come to the throne of grace intelligently understanding what it is that you require. It is good for us in prayer when the Holy Spirit guides the mind. Then let us obey the Holy Spirit and pray as He directs, for He knows what our request should be.

We must remember that He is *"Spirit, and those who worship him must worship in spirit and truth,"* because *"the Father is seeking such people to worship Him"* (John 4:23-24). The first essential of prayer is to pray in truth, and we do not pray in truth unless the Spirit leads our minds into the sincerity and reality of devotion. To pray in truth is this—not to use the empty expression of prayer, but to mean what we say. Only the spiritual person can sigh, desire, and cry in their inmost heart before God, but they cannot do it unless the Spirit of truth leads them in sincerity into the secret of heart-prayer. Praying in the Holy Spirit is praying in passion.

Daily Reflection

The Holy Spirit is crucial to prayer. Without Him, we cannot pray in *spirit* and truth. But often He is misunderstood or neglected, and so our prayer life suffers as a result. The role of the Holy Spirit in our lives, not just prayer, will determine whether we bear spiritual fruit or not. Take time to listen to His still, small voice as you work through these questions.

1. What is the relationship between faith, prayer, love, and hope?
2. What is meant by the sentence, "Only prayer which comes from God can go to God"?

3. How do we test our prayers?
4. What is the connection between spirit and truth when it comes to prayers?
5. Do you find it easy or difficult to pray in the Holy Spirit? Why?

11

ORDER IN PRAYER

"Oh, that I knew where I might find him, that I might come even to his seat! I would lay my case before him and fill my mouth with arguments"
Job 23:3-4

In this verse, Job teaches us how he meant to plead and intercede with God. He reveals the secrets of his prayer room and unveils the art of prayer. If we can become apprentices to Job and have a lesson from his Master, we may gain incredible skill in interceding with God.

Unfortunately, if you want to know what order we should follow in prayer, I am not about to give you a scheme like those that many have drawn up, where adoration, confession, petition, intercession, and ascription are arranged in sequence. I think the true spiritual order of prayer consists of something more than simply arranging it correctly.

Who We Address

The right place for us to start is to first feel that we are doing something that is real. We must know that we are about to address God; whom we cannot see, but who is present; whom we cannot touch or hear, or realize through our senses, but who is with us as if we were speaking to a real flesh-and-blood friend like ourselves. Once we feel the reality of God's presence, our minds will be led by grace into humility; we will feel like Abraham, when he said, *"I have undertaken to speak to the Lord, I who am but dust and ashes"* (Gen 18:27).

Consequently, we will not enter into prayer like children repeating their school lessons through rote learning. We cannot speak as if we were rabbis instructing our pupils or as thieves stopping a person and demanding their money and belongings. Instead, we will be humble yet bold petitioners, humbly asking for mercy through the Savior's blood. We will not have the attitude of a slave but the loving reverence of a child; not a rude, demanding child, but a teachable, obedient child who honors his Father and sincerely asks, but in submission to his Father's will.

When I feel that I am in the presence of God, and take my rightful position there, the next thing I will want to accept is that I have no right to what I am asking, and cannot expect to receive it except as a gift of grace. I need to remember that God limits the means by which He gives me mercy—He will give it to me through His Son. So, let me bring myself under the Redeemer's approval. Let me feel that it is no longer I who am speaking but Christ that is speaking with me and that while I plead, I plead His wounds, His life, His death, His blood, Himself. This is what it means to get into order.

Asking Specifically

The next thing is to consider what I am going to ask for. It is a good thing, when praying, to begin making specific and definite requests. Many of the loud, public prayers we hear are from people who are not really asking God for anything.

It is good not to beat around the bush in prayer, but to come directly to the point. I like that prayer of Abraham's, *"Oh that Ishmael might live before you!"* (Gen 17:18). We can clearly see the name and the person being prayed for, and the blessing that is desired, all in just a few words. Why not be to-the-point and say what we mean as well as mean what we say?

Ordering our case would make us more specific in our minds. It is also not necessary to itemize the catalog of everything that you may need, want, have had, can have, or shall have. Ask for what you need now. As a rule, stick to the present need, ask for your daily bread—what you want now—ask for that. Ask for it clearly, as you are before God who does not care for your exquisite expressions, and who sees your eloquence and speech as nothing but vanity. You are before the Lord, let your words be few, but let your heart be passionate.

Desiring His Will

The ordering of prayer is not quite complete when you have asked for what you want through Jesus Christ—there is more. We should also examine what we are asking for. We might have a hidden motive in our desire which is not Christ-like, a selfish reason, that forgets God's glory and only looks out for our own ease and comfort. Although we may ask for things that are for our good, we must still never let that interfere with the glory of God in any way. Combined with acceptable prayer we should find the holy salt of submission to God's will.

Put these three things together: The deep spirituality that sees prayer as being a real conversation with the invisible God; the reality of prayer in being specific, asking for what we know we want; and with passion, believing the thing to be necessary, and so taking hold of it in complete submission, leaving it with the Master's will—combine all of these, and you have a clear idea of what it means to order your case before the Lord.

Daily Reflection

We can see that it is important to have order in our prayers, but often we can become so ordered, that our prayers slip into formats and lack any kind of life. To understand the order in its right place, we need to pay careful attention to those who have got it right, and we have many examples to learn from! Spurgeon calls it an 'art,' something to be mastered.

1. Spurgeon says there is more to spiritual order than arranging prayer—what is it?
2. What is the secret to approaching God when we pray?
3. Why is it so important to be "specific and definite" in our prayers?
4. What is the connection between asking for something and knowing God's will?
5. How would you rate your prayers in terms of order?

12

BIBLICAL ARGUMENTS TO USE IN PRAYER

"Oh, that I knew where I might find him, that I might come even to his seat! I would lay my case before him and fill my mouth with arguments"
Job 23:3-4

The first question we must ask is, why should arguments be used at all? The arguments are for our own benefit, not for His. He wants us to plead and beg Him, and to bring our strong reasons forward, because, as Isaiah said, this will show that we feel the value of the blessing. When a man looks to argue for something it's because he sees what he is seeking as important.

There's no need for prayer at all as far as God is concerned, but how necessary it is for us on our own account! If we were not compelled to pray, I wonder if we could even live as Christians. If God's mercies came to us without us having to ask for them, they wouldn't be half as useful as they are to us now, when they have to be sought for, because now we get a double blessing; a blessing in obtaining it, and a blessing in seeking it. The very act of prayer is a blessing.

Examples of Arguments

It's good to ask according to **Jehovah's character and abilities**. Abraham did so when he was looking for God's justice. He was begging for Sodom, and said, *"Shall not the Judge of all the earth do what is just?"* (Gen 18:25). When he realized he would not get the justice he was seeking, he reached for God's right hand of mercy. So you and I can also take hold of the justice, mercy, faithfulness, wisdom, patience, and kindness of God, and we'll find each of His characteristics to be a battering ram that can open the gates of heaven.

Another incredible weapon in the battle of prayer is **God's promise**. Jacob begged God not to allow Esau to destroy the women and the children. The main reason he used in his argument was, *"But you said, 'I will surely do you good'"* (Gen 32:12). The strength of that request is amazing! He was holding God to His word, "But you said."

If you have been given a promise from God, you don't need to ask with an 'if' in it; you can plead with certainty. You know His will; that will is in the promise, plead it. Don't let Him rest until He fulfills it. He means to fulfill it, or else He would not have given it. God doesn't give His word to keep us quiet and to keep us hopeful for a while, with the intention of putting us off at the last moment. When He speaks, He speaks because He means to act.

A third argument to be used is **God's reputation**—*"What will you do for your great name?"* (Joshua 7:9). I have told my friends and neighbors that I put my trust in You, and if You do not deliver me now, where is Your name? God, come and do this thing, otherwise, Your honor will be thrown into the dust.

We can also plead with the **sorrow of His people**. This is often done. Jeremiah is the great master of this art. In Lamentations 4, he talks of all their griefs and difficulties in the siege. He calls on the Lord to see the suffering of Zion, and before long his cries were heard.

It's also good to plead with God using **the past** as an argument. Here is David's example: *"O you who have been my help. Cast me not off; forsake me not"* (Psalm 27:9). He pleads for God's mercy from when he was young. He speaks of being chosen by God from when he was born, and then he pleads, *"So even to old age and gray hairs, O God, do not forsake me"* (Psalm 71:18).

We can even use our **own unworthiness** as an argument with God. In one place, David begs, *"O Lord, pardon my guilt, for it is great"* (Psalm 25:11). That is an extraordinary form of reasoning, but being interpreted it means, "Lord, why should You go about doing little things? The greatness of my sin makes me a platform for the greatness of Your mercy. Let the greatness of Your love be seen in me."

Finally, the best Christian argument to use in prayer is the **sufferings, death, merit, and intercession of Jesus.** I am worried that we don't understand the power that we have when we are allowed to plead with God for Jesus' sake.

It would be better if we thought more of Jesus' grief and suffering in our prayers. Bring His wounds before God; remind Him of Jesus' cries and groans from Gethsemane, and let His blood from Calvary speak for itself. Tell God that with such grief, cries, and groans to plead, you can't be denied or rejected. Arguments like these will make sure of it.

Daily Reflection

Using arguments in prayer is one of Spurgeon's favorite topics, and it often comes up in his sermons on prayer. Instead of an actual argument as we understand the word in the context of a quarrel, it means to have a reason to support what you are saying. Using God's words to give our requests more validity makes our prayers stronger and more effective.

1. Do you agree with Spurgeon's statement that prayer and arguments are not for God's benefit?
2. Have you ever used any of these arguments in prayer?
3. Which of these seem normal, and which seem almost arrogant? Why?
4. What is the benefit of using these arguments?

13

THE SECRET POWER IN PRAYER

"If you abide in me, and my words abide in you, ask whatever you wish, and it will be done for you"
John 15:7

One of the first results of our abiding with Christ will be in prayer—'*ask.*' Prayer comes spontaneously from those who abide in Jesus. Just as the leaf and the fruit come out of the vine branch without any conscious effort on the part of the branch, but simply because of its living union with the stem, so prayer buds, blossoms, and fruits out of hearts abiding in Jesus.

The fruit of our abiding is not only prayer, but freedom in prayer, *"ask whatever you wish."* Have you been on your knees without the power to pray? You wanted to pray, but the waters were frozen up and would not flow. The will was present, but not the freedom to present that will in prayer.

"If you abide in me, and my words abide in you, ask whatever you wish." It does not mean that you will have freedom in words and fluency, but freedom of access in prayer.

That's not all. There is also the privilege of successful prayer. *"Ask whatever you wish, and it will be done for you."* You long to bear fruit—ask, and it will be done for you. Look at the vine branch. It simply remains in the vine, and by remaining in the vine the fruit comes from it. It is done for it. *"Delight yourself in the LORD, and he will give you the desires of your heart"* (Psalm 37:4). He puts a signed check into our hands and permits us to fill it as we want.

How can we lack anything if the Lord has said, *"Ask whatever you wish, and it will be done for you"*?

How do we receive this power? The answer is, *"If you abide in me."* Here are the two feet we use to climb to power with God in prayer. We must abide in Him, by always trusting Him and Him only. A temporary faith will not save. An abiding faith is necessary. But abiding in the Lord Jesus does not only mean trusting in Him, it includes surrendering ourselves to Him to receive His life, and to let that life work out its results in us. We live in Him, by Him, for Him, to Him, when we abide in Him.

Jesus says, *"every branch that does bear fruit he prunes"* (John 15:2). Make sure you abide in Christ when you are being pruned and the sharp knife is cutting everything away. Endure trial, and never dream of giving up your faith because of it.

Don't forget the second part of the verse, *"my words abide in you."* How important are Jesus' words! We cannot separate Jesus from the Word, because He is the Word. If you will not have Jesus and His words, He will also not have you nor your words—you will ask in vain and soon give up asking, and become like a withered branch.

If the Word of God abides in you, you are the person that can pray, because you meet God with His own words. This is the best praying in all the world. As you feed on the Word, and are filled with the Word, retain the Word in your faith, and obey the Word in your life, in that proportion you will be skilled in prayer.

If we abide in Jesus, and His words abide in us, then the Holy Spirit has come to live in us, and what better help in prayer can we have? The Spirit knows the mind of God, and He works in us to will what God wills, so that a believing man's prayer is God's purpose reflected in the soul as in a mirror. How clear that if we abide in Christ, and His words abide in us, we can ask what we will, because we will only ask what the Spirit moves us to ask.

John 15:9 says, *"As the Father has loved me, so have I loved you. Abide in my love."* The same love God gives to His Son, the Son gives to us, and so we live in the love of the Father and the Son. How can our prayers be rejected? Will not infinite love respect our request? If you do not abide in Christ, how can you hope to pray successfully? If you pick and choose His words, and doubt this and that, are willfully disobedient to any of His words, will not this mean failure in prayer? But abide in Christ, and hold onto His words, and be His disciple, then you will be heard by Him. Abide in Christ, and let His words abide in you, and then this special privilege will be yours.

Daily Reflection

Abiding in Jesus is a key aspect of Christianity. Many sermons and books have been preached and written on it, what it means, how to do it, and its effect on our lives. For more in-depth teaching, Andrew Murray's *Abide in Christ* is a wonderful book that can further highlight and reveal what this means.

1. In this instance, what is the fruit of abiding in Jesus?
2. What do you understand by the words, *"whatever you wish"*?
3. What are the two 'feet' we use to "climb to power with God in prayer"?
4. Read 1 John 4:13. How does this relate to this reading?

14

ESSENTIAL POINTS IN PRAYER

> *"The Lord appeared to Solomon a second time, as he had appeared to him at Gibeon. And the Lord said to him, "I have heard your prayer and your plea, which you have made before me. I have consecrated this house that you have built, by putting my name there forever. My eyes and my heart will be there for all time"*
> 1 Kings 9:2-3

The Lord spoke to Solomon about his prayer, and there is a lot that makes it a good model for us. In this case, we will follow the Lord's own description of an accepted prayer.

Our Place

God said, *"I have heard your prayer and your plea, which you have made before me."* This is the place to pray—*"before me"*—before the Lord.

The Pharisee went up to the temple to pray, but he did not pray "before God." If you went to pray at Calvary or Gethsemane, you might not actually be before God. Praying before God is more spiritual than turning to the east or the west, or bowing the knee.

"Pour out your heart before him" (Psalm 62:8). *"Before him"* is the place for the heart's outpouring, and those who know and find it are blessed!

Our prayer must be "before God," or else it is not an acceptable prayer. Do you find yourself on your knees repeating words while your heart is wandering? You have not realized His presence, you have not spoken distinctly and directly to Him. The main point is not to pray in the presence of others or your own presence, but to present your prayer "before God."

Lord, deliver us from staying in the words, but bring us into the spirit of prayer, bring us near You. The soul of prayer is being before God, and desiring before God, who hears without sounds, and understands without expressions. You are praying before God when you have realized His presence.

Our Requirement

It is necessary for a living prayer to feel that we are speaking to God and that God is hearing us. David says very little about God's answering, but he always speaks about God's hearing, and he asks that He would hear. The first thing wanted, then, is that the Lord should hear us. But we want more than that, we want that He should accept our prayer. To have brought an offering which the Lord has accepted is the delight of supplication!

Still, there is a third thing that we want, which God gave to Solomon and that was an answer. We need to believe that we have the requests that we ask. We must ask in faith, not doubting, or we may not expect to receive anything from the Lord.

Our Assurance of an Answer

Can we have an assurance that God has heard and answered prayer? Solomon had it. The Lord said, *"I have heard your prayer and your plea."* Does the Lord ever say that to us? If we can trust God, we will have the thing we seek. Faith is not saying, "I know that I have it," when you really do not. That would be telling yourself a lie. There is a difference between believing what you want and believing what God has promised.

Strong faith often brings with it a conviction within the soul that nothing can shake; a sure conviction inspired by the Spirit of God who bears witness only to the truth, and not to dreams. Sometimes God gives us an assurance that He has heard our prayer when He makes us look back and observe the past. How He has answered us! He changes not, He hears us still.

We learn what Solomon's prayer was when we hear how God fulfilled it. God said to him, *"I have consecrated this house that you have built, by putting my name there forever. My eyes and my heart will be there for all time."*

Solomon prayed and God heard him, that the eye of the Lord might be there. That was his prayer, and God improved on it because He said that His eye *and* His heart would always be there. Often the Lord hears our prayers better than the way we offer them. We pray that His eye may be on us, and He adds, "It shall be so, and with my eye, my heart also shall be there."

Daily Reflection

Perhaps, like many people, you have sometimes wondered what a good prayer is, what is acceptable to God, and if your prayer is any good. Using Solomon as an example, we can see an order and a heart behind the type of prayer that God is looking for.

1. How would you describe a living prayer?
2. What do you understand by "before God"? How do you do this?
3. What are the three things that we want or require in a living prayer?

4. Why are assurance, confidence, and faith so important in prayer?
5. How do your own prayers compare to this model?

15

UNANSWERED PRAYERS

"O my God, I cry by day, but you do not answer, and by night, but I find no rest"
Psalm 22:2

These are more Jesus' words than David's. Why was the Savior allowed to go through such an experience? He was making an atonement for us and He was not heard because we as sinners did not deserve to be heard. But, there was also another reason—that He might be a faithful High Priest having sympathy with His people in their troubles. Not being heard in prayer, or being unanswered for a while, is one of the greatest troubles that Christians experience.

Jesus humbled Himself and became obedient to His Father's will. His faith never staggered. His confidence in His God never turned into suspicion or unbelief. In this, He not only sympathizes with us, but He sets us an example. We must overcome, as He did, through faith. *"And this is the victory that has overcome the world—our faith"* (1 John 5:4). If we can copy Him, we will triumph as He overcame.

When Prayers Are Not Answered

In the first place, the verse teaches us that we must **not stop trusting** God. *"O my God."* Do not be tempted to give up on your only strength and hope. Say the words of the Psalm, *"Yet you are holy"* (Psalm 22:3). Settle that in your mind. He is true. He is faithful. Even in the worst case, He delivered His Son and came through, and in every other case, He has done the same.

Just as we are not to stop trusting, so we are **not to cease praying**. The verse is on this: *"I cry in the daytime, but You do not hear; And in the night season, and am not silent"* (NKJV). Not every knock at mercy's gate opens it. The person that succeeds must knock again, and again, and again. Bring your prayers like a battering ram against the gate of heaven and force it open with a holy violence, *"the kingdom of heaven has suffered violence, and the violent take it by force"* (Matt. 11:12).

We must also **not stop hoping**. If you have prayed for a long time, continue to hope. There is a phrase, "the swimming-thought," which means that when all other thoughts have drowned, hope still swims, lifts her head above the waves, and sees the blue heaven above her and hopes. *"Hope in God; for I shall again praise him, my salvation and my God"* (Psalm 42:11). As long as there is a place of prayer and a promise of an answer, no believer ought to give way to despair.

Continue to trust. Continue to pray. Increase in your persistence and in the hope that the blessing will still come.

Why Prayers Are Not Answered

Unanswered prayer should be a search warrant for every Christian, and we should begin examining ourselves to see if there is anything that is contrary to the will of God. *"Search me, O God, and know my heart! Try me and know my thoughts! And see if there be any grievous way in me, and lead me in the way everlasting!"* (Psalm 139:23-24). I think this is one great reason for unanswered prayer—discipline for sin.

Sometimes, there is **sin in the prayer itself**. We are children, and we must remember how we should speak to our Father. We must not mistake the familiarity of communion for being disrespectful.

Sometimes, if a blessing came immediately when we asked for it, **it might be too soon**; God times it until it comes at the right and best moment. You have asked for an adult's trials, privileges, and work, but you are still a child growing up into an adult. If it came now, it might involve responsibilities that you could not handle, but at the right time, you will be prepared for it.

Sometimes, delays in prayer are **a training school** for us. Look at Paul's example. The "thorn in the flesh" was very painful, and even though he was a chosen apostle, he did not receive the answer he was waiting for. In these moments, God is strengthening your muscles by the tough exercise of unanswered prayer, so that you may be useful in the future.

Perhaps the reason why prayer is not always quickly answered is that **only God knows**! Who am I that I should question Him as to what He does? Am I the Potter or the clay? Leave these things with God, and go on with your praying and your believing, and everything will be well with you.

Daily Reflection

As Spurgeon says, unanswered prayers are one of our greatest troubles—it is a common problem across the board. In tackling this issue, he unlocks some practical elements that can help us identify times and attitudes that could have resulted in not hearing from God. Be honest as you go through the reflections, as this is how you will be able to see areas that need attention, growth, and the Holy Spirit's help.

1. Do you find it surprising that the words of the verse are accredited to Jesus?
2. Which of the three instances of when prayers are unanswered pertain to you?
3. Have you ever prayed the words of Psalm 139:23-24 for yourself? What happened?
4. Have you ever experienced any of the four reasons why prayers are unanswered?

16

BRIEF AND SILENT PRAYER

"So I prayed to the God of heaven"
Nehemiah 2:4

There are three thoughts that I intend to look at in detail: The fact that Nehemiah prayed at that moment, the manner of his prayer, and the kind of prayer he used.

Nehemiah Prays

He had been asked a question by his king. The proper thing would be to answer it. Before Nehemiah answered, he prayed to God. I am not sure the king noticed the pause. Maybe the interval was not long enough to be noticed, but it was long enough for God to notice it—long enough for Nehemiah to have sought and found guidance from God on how to answer the king.

The king asks him what he wants, and his whole heart is set on building up Jerusalem. Are you not surprised that he did not immediately say, "Oh king, live forever. I long to build up Jerusalem's walls. Give me all the help you can"? But, as eager as he was to take hold of his goal, he kept his hand back until he prayed to the God of heaven. I admire him. I also want to imitate him.

It's even more surprising that Nehemiah should have prayed at that moment because he had been already praying for the past three or four months about the same matter. But, the person who has prayed much is the person who will pray even more.

There is one more thing worth looking at: He was doing his job in the court, standing before the king to give him the golden goblet, and he did not answer the king's question until he had first prayed to the God of heaven.

The Manner of Prayer

This was what we call a brief prayer—prayer that throws a dart and then it is done. It was not the prayer that stood knocking at mercy's door, but it was the concentration of many knocks in one. I see this brief, quick prayer as one of the very best forms of prayer.

Notice how short it must have been. It was introduced—slipped in—sandwiched in—between the king's question and

Nehemiah's answer. And as I have already said, I don't think it took up any time at all—hardly a second.

We also know that it must have been a silent prayer, and not just silent in terms of sound, but silent in the heart—perfectly secret.

The Style of Praying

The duty and privilege of every Christian are to have set times of prayer. It is good for your heart, memory, and moral consistency to schedule in portions of time and say, "These belong to God. I will do business with God at this time, and try to be as punctual with Him as if I had made an engagement to meet a friend."

But I also want to emphasize the value of short, brief, quick, frequent prayers like the one we saw Nehemiah use. And I recommend this because it is no obstacle to engagements and does not take up much time. You may be measuring off your curtains, weighing your groceries, or you may be drawing up an account, and between the items, you may say, "Lord, help me." You may breathe a prayer to heaven and say, "Lord, keep me." It will take no time.

The habit of prayer is blessed, but the spirit of prayer is better, and the spirit of prayer is the mother of these brief silent prayers. Many times in a day we can speak with the Lord our God.

These prayers are commendable because they are truly spiritual. Wordy prayers can also be windy prayers. There is a lot of praying by the book that is not recommended as it is empty. The prayers that come leaping out of the heart—the gust of strong emotion, passionate desire, lively faith—these are truly spiritual, and God won't accept any prayers but spiritual prayers.

This kind of prayer is also free from the corrupt motive of being said in order to please others. They cannot say that the secret, brief, silent prayers of our heart are presented to receive our own praise, for no one knows that we are praying at all.

The habit of offering these brief prayers will also keep a check on your confidence in yourself. It will show your dependence on God. It will keep you from becoming worldly. It will be like a sweet perfume burnt in your heart to keep out the fever of the world. I can strongly recommend these short, sweet, blessed prayers. May the Holy Spirit give them to you!

Daily Reflection

This is Spurgeon at his practical best, giving us a method of praying that is not only possible to fit into our busy schedules, but is also just as effective. By using a biblical example, we can see the context and the outcome of the prayer, and how we can use the same practice in our own lives.

1. Why do you think Nehemiah prayed again, even though he had already prayed for this specific thing?
2. Do brief, silent prayers line up with what it says in 1 Thessalonians 5:17?

3. Do you find it easy to stick to set times of prayer in your life?
4. What is the difference between the habit and the spirit of prayer?
5. Do brief, silent prayers rule out the need for long prayers?

17

PRAYING AND WAITING

"I write these things to you who believe in the name of the Son of God, that you may know that you have eternal life. And this is the confidence that we have toward him, that if we ask anything according to his will he hears us. And if we know that he hears us in whatever we ask, we know that we have the requests that we have asked of him"
1 John 5:13-15

Knowing

John writes to the people as believers who have eternal life. But it is one thing to have eternal life and another thing to know that we have eternal life. He draws a distinction between knowing Jesus and knowing that we know Him, for he writes, *"And by this we know that we have come to know him, if we keep his commandments"* (1 John 2:3). A person might know Jesus in his heart, and yet at certain seasons, through weakness of judgment, or stress of temptations, he may have doubts as to whether he has any knowledge of Jesus at all.

I know faith is confidence concerning the truth of God. I accept the definition, but I want you to see that there is a difference between being sure of the truth of God, and being sure that we can enter into that life. You may believe in Jesus and have eternal life, and still doubt it. John wants us to believe so that we can reach a higher state of faith, and may know without a doubt that we have eternal life.

Just continue to believe as you have believed. Receive the Word of God as it stands. You do not want any other reason for assurance except what is written there, and the Spirit will help you to see your own calling, sealed and sure. Continue to rest in Jesus, and you will find that in Him, as you have found faith, so you will also have an assurance of faith. This is the first of three steps that he wants to lead us up.

Confidence

John then leads us to a second rung of the ladder: *"And this is the confidence that we have toward him, that if we ask anything according to his will he hears us."* From the confidence we now have in Christ, the next step is to a strong belief in the power of prayer.

God acknowledges your prayer, and this would not be so unless you had received the confidence of your own calling in Him, because belief in the power of prayer depends on your conviction of being in Christ. Paul's argument is, *"He who did not spare his own Son but gave him up for us all, how will he not also with him graciously give us all things?"* (Rom. 8:32). I must be sure that God has given me Jesus, and if He has given me Jesus, then I know that He will give me all things. But if I have any doubt about Jesus being mine, and about me being able to receive God's gift in Jesus, I cannot say the same words as Paul. I also cannot have confidence that my prayer is heard.

God's Fatherhood is another reason for our confidence in prayer. *"If you then, who are evil, know how to give good gifts to your children, how much more will the heavenly Father give the Holy Spirit to those who ask him!"* (Luke 11:13). But if I am not clear that God is my Father, if I do not have the spirit of adoption, then I cannot come to God with this confidence that He will give me my desire. If I am confident in my sonship, I am confident that my Father knows what I need and will hear me.

Conviction

If you have climbed this second step, then the third is not difficult. It is to go from your belief that God hears prayer, to a conviction that when you have prayed you have the request that you have desired of him. *"And if we know that he hears us in whatever we ask, we know that we have the requests that we have asked of him."* To move from a conviction that prayer works, to believe that when you have desired anything of God in prayer, through Jesus, you have received the answer.

We have heaven, but we cannot enjoy it yet. We also might have answers to our prayers, but as far as we can see, we have not received anything. We have it, but we do not see it. It is ours, but God sees fit to keep it for a season to test our faith. We might have the answers to many of our prayers, really have the answers, but for now, that answer, like a ship on a long journey, might not have returned yet.

We must know that having sought the Lord in prayer through Jesus, we have the requests that we asked of Him. I want to encourage us to look for answers to prayer. Seeing that you have the promise of an answer to prayer and that the answer must come to you, look for it. Unless you believe that you have the answer in reality, you will not look for its appearance, but if you have come so far as to believe that you have the answer, I encourage you to look for it and rejoice.

Daily Reflection

Waiting is one of the hardest things humans have to learn to do, especially in a world that rewards speed, efficiency, and productivity. Yet, all through the Bible God tells us to wait, and to do it patiently. Prayer is no different—we often seem to have to wait for answers. Spurgeon's direction and encouragement in this area are so helpful.

1. Explain the difference between 'having' and 'knowing.'
2. How does knowing something bring us to have the confidence we need in prayer?

3. Why should God the Father give us confidence in prayer?
4. How does conviction help us to wait?
5. Read Psalm 37. Notice the three different rungs of the ladder, as well as the number of times we are told to wait for God.

18

A GOLDEN PRAYER

"Father, glorify your name"
John 12:28

These words come just after Jesus raised Lazarus from the dead. The miracle had attracted many, enthusiastic crowds gathered, and He had become so popular that the Pharisees said, *"Everyone will believe in him"* (John 11:48). Even Greeks came and asked to be introduced to Him. If they expected to see a king, they saw instead a man in grief. Jesus was troubled. He felt a premonition of that midnight among the olives, in which His soul was *"very sorrowful, even to death"* (Matt. 26:38).

The Master of all worlds, supreme among the angels, and adored at His Father's right hand, says, *"Now is my soul trou-*

bled" (John 12:27). Have you ever cried out that your heart is troubled? Then remember that Jesus used the same words. Are you distracted in your thoughts? Do you look around and feel that you do not know what to do, and you pray, *"Father, save me from this hour"* (John 12:27)? With the same afflictions, He has been afflicted.

There may be a struggle in the soul and yet the Father may be glorified, the sin lies not in the conflict but the defeat. *"If it be possible, let this cup pass from me,"* is not sinful if it is followed by, *"nevertheless, not as I will, but as you will"* (Matt. 26:39) Jesus did not dishonor the Father by saying, *"Now is my soul troubled."* He wept, and we may weep. He told His sorrow to His friends and you may do the same.

Look at the question He asked, *"Now is my soul troubled. And what shall I say? 'Father, save me from this hour'?"* and see how it was really answered in His heart before He asked it—"Father, glorify Your name by My death." His first prayer is not, "Father, save my people," but, *"Father, glorify your name."* The glory of God was the goal and objective of our Savior's life and death.

May this verse also be our prayer, *"Father, glorify your name."* Have you ever prayed this prayer?

This verse means that the conflict inside you has ended. When you can pray, *"Father, glorify your name,"* then there is no more question about, *"What shall I say?"* You have said the right thing, so leave it there. When you pray like this, your conflict is over, no fear remains. If that prayer comes from the heart, you have cast aside all fear and worry, and you can carry on into the unknown tomorrow.

Secondly, our verse indicates the surrender of self. When we can truly say, *"Father, glorify your name,"* we begin to understand the saying of Jesus concerning the corn of wheat falling into the ground and dying. The prayer means that I am willing to be made nothing so that Your will may be done. I am willing to be like someone dead and buried, forgotten and unknown, if You will be magnified.

This surrender includes obedient service, for Jesus goes on to say, *"If anyone serves me, the Father will honor him."* True self-renunciation shows itself in obediently imitating Jesus. *"Father, glorify your name"* means waiting for the Lord's call and running in His ways.

Saying this prayer—*"Father, glorify your name"*—is the same as saying, if I must lose my property, glorify Your name in my poverty; if I must be bereaved, glorify Your name in my sorrows; if I must die, glorify Your name in my departure.

How can I struggle against that which is really glorifying my Father? Your heart will stop questioning and being afraid, and stay safe beneath the eternal wings, in deep peace. Filled with patience, you will take the cup, and grasp it with willingness and eagerness. "It is to glorify God," you will say, "Every drop of this cup is for His glory," and so you will put it to your mouth and drink again and again, and again until you have drunk the last drop, and find that *"It is finished"* (John 19:30).

I know you will not fail to do this if your heart has really felt the power of this prayer—*"Father, glorify your name."*

Daily Reflection

Having a notebook and pen will help in these reflections rather than just verbally going through them. Writing down thoughts, answers, and ideas will not only help you to commit yourself to work through the questions, but you will be able to review them later. You may see growth in areas or issues that you still want to work on.

1. Do you bring your conflicts to God in prayer?
2. Do you ever think that your times of trouble can be used to glorify God? Is it ever a prayer of yours?
3. What part of surrendering yourself do you find the hardest?
4. Read Psalm 115:1 and Romans 12:1. What do you understand by these verses in the light of the reading?

19

PRAYER MEETINGS

"All these with one accord were devoting themselves to prayer"
Acts 1:14

In the Early Church

The first prayer meeting we find after Jesus ascended to heaven is mentioned in our verse, and we can see that united prayer is a **comfort for a hurting church**. Nothing strengthened them to bear their difficulties so much as to draw near to God in common prayer.

In Acts 2, we see that prayer meetings are the **place to receive spiritual power**; *"they were all together in one place"* (Acts 2:1) praying, and they heard a mighty wind, tongues of fire came on them, and they were filled with power. If we want the power of the Holy Spirit, we will find it in the prayer meeting.

In Acts 4, we see that prayer meetings are the **resource of a persecuted church**. Peter and John were in prison and *"And when they had prayed, the place in which they were gathered together was shaken, and they were all filled with the Holy Spirit and continued to speak the word of God with boldness. Now the full number of those who believed were of one heart and soul"* (Acts 4:31-32). Persecuting times are often good for the church because they compel us to pray.

In Acts 12, we find the prayer meeting was a **place for individual deliverance**. Peter was in prison sleeping, but the church prayed for him, and he was set free. When we come together, we can unite in specific and personal prayers.

In Acts 13:2, there is a prayer meeting that mentions **mission work**. While they were fasting in prayer, the Holy Spirit said, *"Set apart for me Barnabas and Saul for the work to which I have called them,"* so they laid their hands on them, and sent them away.

Why Have Them?

The prayer meeting is useful for the answer it gets from God, but it is also useful for other things.

We sing together and pray together, and our Christian fellowship is shown to the world and becomes sweeter for ourselves. Some people may be dull and heavy, but others who are passionate and lively can stimulate and excite them. There is a spiritual enthusiasm that sometimes comes to us at the prayer meeting.

United prayer is useful where God has promised extraordinary blessings:

- *"where two or three are gathered in my name, there am I among them"* (Matt. 18:20).
- *"if two of you agree on earth about anything they ask, it will be done for them by my Father in heaven"* (Matt. 18:19).

God asks for agreement and once we agree, He promises that the prayer will be answered.

It is in the spirit of prayer that our strength lies.

Obstacles

There are some obstacles to prayer before people come to a meeting.

Unholiness blocks prayer. A person cannot walk contrary to God and then expect to have their prayers heard. When Christians do not agree with each other, they do not really love one another and then their prayers cannot succeed. Discord spoils prayer, and so does hypocrisy.

But there are some things that block the prayer meeting when we are at it. One is long prayers. It is terrible to hear someone pray us into a good attitude of prayer, and then, by their long prayer, pray us out of it again. Or when they do not pray, but preach a short sermon, and tell the Lord all about themselves, instead of just asking for what they want.

Prayer meetings are often hindered by a lack of directness and by beating about the bush. We must not come with well-rounded and polished sentences, but to pray, praise, confess, and find cleansing. And if we do this, the prayer meeting will not disappoint us.

Prayer meetings are sometimes blocked by a lack of sincerity in those who pray, and in those who pray in silence. It is possible for us to attend the meeting but be thinking of the home, children, shop, work, and so many other things. The person who prays may be burning with a sincere desire, but his prayer is held up because we are not backing it with silent passionate longing for God's blessing.

The prayer meeting can also be spoiled afterward when we ask for a blessing and then don't expect to receive it. If our faith is nothing, then the answer will also be nothing. Not practically carrying out our desires will also spoil the prayer meeting. If we ask God to convert people but do nothing for those souls. If we ask God to save your children, but don't talk to them about their salvation. You pray for fruit, but you will not put out your hand to pluck it, and all this spoils the prayer meeting. Sincere prayer should always be followed up by persevering efforts and then the result will be great indeed.

Daily Reflection

Prayer meetings seem to be a part of every church's life, often attended by only a few faithful members. Most times, wrongly, they are regarded as an addition to the real heart of the church. Pastors tend to have to invent ways to get more people to join or encourage them to see the importance of the meetings.

1. Do you ever attend prayer meetings?
2. Do you find them enriching and powerful times or are they boring, tedious, and something to be ticked off as part of our duty?
3. Have you ever thought that the strength of the church lies in prayer meetings? How strong is your church based on this?
4. Have you ever experienced some of these issues that block prayer in a meeting?

20

PRAY WITHOUT CEASING

"Pray without ceasing"
1 Thessalonians 5:17

The position of our verse is very suggestive. It comes immediately after the command, *"Rejoice always"* (1 Thess. 5:16). It's as if we asked, "How can I always rejoice?" And Paul gave the answer, "Always pray." The more praying, the more rejoicing.

Since we are to pray without ceasing but cannot always use our voice, it is clear that audible language is not essential to prayer. We can speak a thousand words that seem to be prayer, and yet never pray. We can cry to God effectively, and yet never say a word. God asks Moses, *"Why do you cry to me?"* (Ex. 14:15). And yet there is no record of Moses saying a single syllable. I find that I can pray best on my own if I can hear my own voice, but it is not essential. Silence in devotion is as good as words.

The posture of prayer is also not important. If God meant us to be on our knees without ceasing, He would have made the body differently. It is good to pray on your knees, as it expresses humility, but people have also prayed while flat on their faces, sitting, or standing.

The place is also not essential to prayer, for if there were only certain holy places where prayer was acceptable, churches would need to be extremely large so that we can always live in them. But a specific place has little to do with prayer, as we can see in Paul's words on Mars' Hill, *"The God who made the world and everything in it, being Lord of heaven and earth, does not live in temples made by man"* (Acts 17:24).

There is also no time in which prayer is more acceptable or more proper than others. If I am to pray without ceasing, then every second must be suitable for prayer. It is good to have your times of prayer and set apart seasons for special supplication, but we must remember that wherever we seek the Lord with true hearts, He is found by us. Whenever we cry to Him, He hears us. Every place is holy ground to a holy heart, and every day is a holy day to a holy person.

Then what does *"pray without ceasing"* mean? First, it is a privilege. Secondly, a command. You have permission to come to the mercy seat when you want, because the veil of the Most Holy place is torn in two, and our access is indisputable. We have permission to pour out our hearts at all times before the Lord. Nothing can set a barrier between a praying soul and its God.

However, it is still a command, *"Pray without ceasing."*

It means, first, **never abandon prayer**. Do not think you must pray until you are saved and can then stop. To persevere in grace, you must persevere in prayer. Do not abandon the mercy seat for any reason. Never, never, never renounce the habit of prayer or your confidence in its power.

A second meaning is—**never stop regular prayer**. Keep up your daily prayer without breaking it. I know a blind person who has been begging without ceasing. He has not begged when he has been asleep or when he has gone home to eat. So, when it is proper for you to leave your normal tasks, you continue begging at mercy's throne; it would be right that you are praying without ceasing.

Thirdly, **between times of devotion, try spontaneous, brief prayers**. While your hands are busy with the world, let your hearts still talk with God in short sentences. The person who prays without ceasing uses many little darts and hand grenades of godly desire which they throw at every available moment.

Fourthly, **we must always be in the spirit of prayer**. Our heart, renewed by the Holy Spirit, must be like the magnetized needle which is always drawn toward the pole. So let your heart be magnetized with prayer so that if your duty turns you away from the actual prayer, the longing desire for prayer is still in your soul. As perfume lies in flowers even when they do not shed their fragrance upon the gale, so let prayer lie in your hearts.

The last meaning of this verse is to **let your actions be consistent with your prayers**. We must pursue our prayers, but do it in another manner. The person who prays for others, and then does good for them, is still praying. Loving is praying. If I seek God's glory above everything, then if all my actions are meant to tend to God's glory, I am continuing to pray, even though I may not be praying with my thoughts or with my mouth. Let your whole life be praying.

Daily Reflection

"Pray without ceasing" is a command we accept along with "love one another." Yet, it is another thing to actually bring ourselves to be able to accomplish them properly with the right attitude. We often have our own definition of the phrase, "without ceasing," to make it easier to fit into our busy daily lives. But Spurgeon is very clear on what it means and practical on how to get it right.

1. What does rejoicing have to do with praying?
2. If our voice, position, place, and time do not restrict us in prayer, what is stopping us?
3. Do you see prayer more as a privilege or a command?
4. Which of the five meanings do you agree with most? Which one do you struggle to accept?
5. How do these verses emphasize the same meaning: Romans 12:12, Colossians 4:2?

21

ASK AND HAVE

"You desire and do not have, so you murder. You covet and cannot obtain, so you fight and quarrel. You do not have, because you do not ask. You ask and do not receive, because you ask wrongly, to spend it on your passions"
James 4:2-3

The lusts of evil people develop into arguments; it kills, and desires to have, fights and wars, while the desire of the righteous is guided to express itself in passionate, persistent prayer.

According to the human mind, the only way to get something is to fight for it, and James sets this down as the reason for all fighting. "What causes quarrels and what causes fights *among you? Is it not this, that your passions are at war within you?"* (James 4:1).

Many people live for themselves, competing and warring, fighting for their own with perseverance. If you are to win, you must fight, and everything is fair in war. James says, *"You desire and do not have, so you murder. You covet and cannot obtain, so you fight and quarrel."* When people are consumed by their selfish purposes and do not succeed, they might realize it is *"because you do not ask."*

So why not ask? Because it is unnatural to the natural man to pray. God's reliance he does not understand, self-reliance is his word. Self is his god, and to his god, he looks for success.

For a while, he goes on fighting and warring, but after a while changes his mind. His purpose is the same, but if it cannot be achieved one way, he will try another. If he must ask, then he will ask, and he will become religious. He sees that some religious people prosper in the world and that even sincere Christians are good at business, so he will try their plan.

This is James' criticism—*"You ask and do not receive."* The reason is that his asking is just a format, his heart is not involved. He is asking incorrectly because it is entirely for himself. He wants to prosper to enjoy himself, he wants to be great simply to be admired, his prayer begins and ends with self. He asks God to be his servant and gratify his desires. This prayer is blasphemous.

. . .

WHAT IS the reason Christians do not have a blessing? *"Because you do not ask."* There are Christians who do not ask. A house without prayer is a house without a roof. We cannot expect blessings in our churches if there is none in our families.

But some reply, "There are prayer meetings, and we do ask for the blessing, but it does not come." The answer is the same—*"You ask and do not receive, because you ask wrongly."* When prayer becomes a ritual, is cold and chill, then nothing will come of it. We cannot commune with God, who is a consuming fire, if there is no fire in our prayers. Prayers filled with doubt are requests for refusal.

Can the children of God have the same jealousies and ambitions as people of the world? Then the prayers that seek success will not be accepted at the mercy seat. God will not hear us, because *"you ask wrongly."*

Whether we like it or not, asking is the rule of the kingdom. *"Ask, and it will be given to you"* (Matt. 7:7). God will bless Elijah and send rain on Israel, but Elijah must pray for it. If Israel is to prosper, Samuel must plead for it. If the Jews are to be delivered, Daniel must intercede. God will bless Paul, and the nations shall be converted through him, but Paul must pray.

You cannot get the Holy Spirit without prayer. Neither can you get communion with God without prayer. Prayer is the great door of spiritual blessing, and if you close it, you shut out the blessings.

God is willing to give us infinitely more than we ask. I believe that we will have inconceivable blessings if we are ready to pray now.

Daily Reflection

Many of us know the mechanisms of prayer. We know that we must ask and receive, but somehow we struggle to get the parts to work together, or our prayer cogs need some oil to function more smoothly as a unit. Spurgeon's direct and simple approach might seem black-and-white, but that is often the tool we need to jolt us back into action.

1. Why is it "unnatural to the natural man to pray"?
2. What does it mean to *"ask wrongly"*?
3. Why is it not enough just to ask?
4. Spurgeon makes two bold statements: "You cannot get the Holy Spirit without prayer. Neither can you get communion with God without prayer." Do you agree with these?

22

HINDRANCES TO PRAYER

"That your prayers may not be hindered"
1 Peter 3:7

Hindered *From* Prayer

When a person becomes **cold, indifferent, and careless**, one of the first things that suffers is their devotion. Prayer is the true gauge of spiritual power. If your prayers are *"hindered,"* there is something in your spiritual system that needs to be removed, or something lacking that needs to be supplied. *"Keep your heart with all vigilance, for from it flow the springs of life"* (Prov. 4:23), and prayers are among those.

Prayers can be hindered by having **too much to do**. The rich man in the parable had no time for prayer because he was busy planning new barns to store his goods. We can even have too much to do in the church, and this restricts our prayers, like Martha, burdened with serving. The more we do, the more we should pray, and prayer should balance our service.

Prayer is also hindered by having **too little to do**. People who have nothing to do generally do it with lots of fuss. Having nothing to do, they are hired by Satan to hinder and injure others.

Some people hinder their prayers because their **lives have no order**. They get up too late and they have to chase all day, always in a rush. I wish you would each keep a diary of how you pray next week, and see how much, or rather how little, time you spend with God out of the 24 hours.

Hindered *in* Prayer

Some people are hindered in prayer by choosing **the wrong time and place**. Give God and prayer those times when you can be free from interruption. *"But when you pray, go into your room and shut the door and pray to your Father who is in secret. And your Father who sees in secret will reward you"* (Matt. 6:6).

Worrying about things can be a hindrance to prayer. We should cast our care on God who *"cares for you"* (1 Pet. 5:7). To take everything from God's hands and to trust everything in God's hands is a happy way to live and very helpful to prayer. More grace and less worry! More praying and less hoarding! More intercession and less speculating!

Earthly pleasures are the worst of hindrances. How can you follow after things of the world and keep communion with

God? Whatever is not of faith is sin and will block your prayers.

Prayers can also be hindered by **worldly sorrow**. The sorrow that prevents us from praying is rebellion against the will of God. Jesus was *"very sorrowful, even to death"* (Matt. 26:38), but He still prayed. Godly sorrow will drive us to prayer, not away from it.

There are times when prayer is hindered by **a bad temper**. I cannot be effective in prayer if I feel anger in my heart. Jesus gave us good advice: *"leave your gift there before the altar and go. First be reconciled to your brother, and then come and offer your gift"* (Matt. 5:24). We cannot expect to be heard in prayer while grudges pollute our hearts.

Prayer can be hindered if we **dishonor God**—If we dishonor the Father *to whom* we pray, or the Son *through whom* we pray, or the Holy Spirit *by whom* we pray.

Hindered From Effective Praying

First, there must be right living—**obedience**—if our prayers are to succeed with God. *"The prayer of a righteous person has great power as it is working"* (James 5:16). If you do not do Jesus' will, He will not do your will. First, wash in the fountain of atoning grace and have your heart cleansed by the Holy Spirit, or else you cannot succeed in prayer.

In addition to obedience, there must be **faith**. The prayer which succeeds with God is the prayer of someone who believes God will hear them and so they ask with confidence.

Without faith, it is impossible to please God in prayer or anything else.

Third, there must be **holy desires**, or else prayer will be a failure. Those desires must be founded on a promise. If you cannot find that God has promised a blessing, you have no right to ask for it and no reason to expect it.

If prayer is to be effective, there must also be **passion and persistence**. There must be eagerness, intensity—pouring out our hearts before God.

There must also be **a desire for God's glory**. We must desire what we ask because we believe it will glorify God to give it to us. *"Delight yourself in the LORD, and he will give you the desires of your heart"* (Psalm 37:4).

Daily Reflection

In every Christian's prayer life, we feel as though we have hit a wall. Something is blocking us from going forward or seeing the effect of our prayers. Attitudes of the hearts, distractions, and many other things creep in, often unseen, and blunt the end of our weapon. Spurgeon gets practical and lists these things so that we can identify them and sharpen our hearts.

1. What is the difference between hindered *from* and hindered *in*?
2. If you are honest with yourself, which of these hindrances affect you the most?
3. What can you do to overcome them?

4. In this reading, Spurgeon seems to make a distinction between normal prayer and effective, powerful prayer. Which one do your prayers often fall into?
5. Is anything holding you back from effective praying?

23

KNOCK

"Knock, and it will be opened to you"
Matthew 7:7

You can ask and receive, you can seek and find, but you cannot knock and open—the Lord must open the door, or you are shut out forever. God is ready to open the door.

If the door stood wide open, there would be no need to knock. Maybe you think the gate is closed because you feel that you have offended God. If you had enough faith, you would enter in right now, because it is written, *"Whoever comes to me I will never cast out"* (John 6:37).

The door can also be closed and kept shut by unbelief. If you believe, you enter into Jesus, *"Whoever believes in the Son has eternal life"* (John 3:36). But we also read that *"they were unable to enter because of unbelief"* (Heb. 3:19). For 40 years the Israelites were in the desert, yet they never reached the promised land because of unbelief. Is it the same for us? Coming and going, hearing sermons, doing everything right, and joining in worship, but we never enter in because of unbelief.

Do you sometimes complain that you have to knock? It is God's rule. Making us knock is a blessing to us—a school where we must plead with God for a while without seeing any success. We are increasing our capacity for the future. If you knock with a heavy heart, you will sing with joy when it is opened, so do not be discouraged because you stand before a closed door.

God's doors are meant to open. When the verse says, *"Knock, and it will be opened to you,"* it teaches us that the way of gaining entrance to the blessing is simple and available for everyone. Is there a person who cannot put words together in prayer? Never mind, knocking can be done by someone who is not eloquent. If you say "I am not well educated," never mind, a person can knock even though they are not a philosopher or professor. A mute person, a blind person, or a person with an injured, sick hand can knock.

Seek God with all your heart, soul, and strength, through Jesus, and the door of His mercy will open to you. It is a door that seems closed, but because it is a door, it is capable of being opened.

God has also provided a knocker on the door to assist us. What is this knocker? It is the promises of God. It is good to say to God, "Do as You have said." God's promises are bills of exchange, and He will honor them.

Remember that this promise was given freely. You did not come and ask for a promise to be heard in prayer. Do you think God will tantalize us for the mere sake of disappointing us? Will He tell you to knock by His promise, and then laugh at you? No! You can knock, and expect to see the door open.

If you are growing tired and weak, read the promise, and grow strong again. *"Knock, and it will be opened to you."* Look how plain and positive the word *'will'* shines in the middle. In the middle of all the darkness that surrounds you are these words, *"it will be opened to you."*

The great knocker, however, is the name of Jesus. When we go to God and plead the name of Jesus, it means that we plead His authority, that we ask God as though we were in Jesus' place, and expect Him to give it to us as if He were giving it to Jesus. That is more than pleading for Jesus' sake. The apostles did plead with God for Jesus' sake, but he said to them, *"Until now you have asked nothing in my name"* (John 16:24). It is a higher level of prayer, and when we plead His name with the Father, then we succeed amazingly.

God will open the door, and no man can close it. Do not hesitate to enter in. When, in answer to your knocking, you see the door move, then get up, and do not wait any longer. Remember that the opening of that door will not only give you entrance, but it will ensure your safety.

Some people think if they have begun to pray, and are sincere, that this is enough. Praying is not the end, it is only a means. Knocking is not the ultimatum—you must enter in. You must enter by the door or else knocking will all be in vain. Knocking is only the way of entrance, but if you stop at knocking, it is useless. The most sincere, persistent praying is only a way of getting to Jesus. You must enter in.

Daily Reflection

We all know the words: ask, seek, and knock. Spurgeon opens our eyes to see that there is more to this than words like a nursery rhyme. By focusing on the 'knock,' he unlocks a much more active aspect of prayer that we must engage in to become effective and see answers.

1. What is the difference between asking, seeking, and knocking?
2. What is God's rule?
3. Why are the 'knockers' very powerful in assisting us in getting the door to open?
4. Read Luke 18:1-8. How does this story tie in with the reading?
5. Why is knocking not enough?

24

THE PROOF OF GODLINESS

"Therefore let everyone who is godly offer prayer to you at a time when you may be found"
Psalm 32:6

Not everyone is godly, and all those who are godly, are not equally so. The person who finds God everywhere, who looks to God for everything, who could not live without his God, to whom God is his exceeding joy, who dwells in God—this is the godly person.

A Test

The verse is a test to tell whether we are godly or not. In these words, *"Therefore let everyone who is godly offer prayer,"* we have the first sign of a godly person. They pray unto God.

When a person is beginning to be godly, this is the first sign of the change that is being worked in him, *"Behold, he is praying"* (Acts 9:11). Prayer is the breath of life in the newborn believer. If he does not pray, you may suspect that he has only a name to live and that he lacks true spiritual life. And as prayer is the mark of godliness in its infancy, it is equally the mark of godliness in all stages of its growth. The man who has much grace will pray much. If you pray less than you once did, then judge yourself to be less devout, to be less in fellowship with God, to be, in fact, less godly.

There is no better thermometer for your spiritual temperature than this, the measure of the intensity of your prayer. I am not speaking about the quantity of it, for there are some who, for a pretense, make long prayers, but I am speaking about the reality of it, the intensity of it. Prayer is best measured by weight rather than by length and breadth.

A Motive

In the verse, we see a strong motive for praying. The context is, *"I acknowledged my sin to you, and I did not cover my iniquity; I said, "I will confess my transgressions to the LORD," and you forgave the iniquity of my sin"* (Psalm 32:5). God heard the prayer of a great sinner. So God gives us a case like David's so that every one that is godly can pray to Him when they realize their sin.

Another motive for prayer the verse brings us is that we all need forgiveness daily, *"Therefore let everyone who is godly offer prayer."* 'Therefore'—for this covering of sin, for this blotting out of iniquity. *"Forgive us our sins"* (Luke 11:4). What is the need for that request if we have no sins to be forgiven? But therefore, for the forgiveness of sin, everyone who is godly will pray to the Lord.

The word *'therefore'* also means, "Because God hears prayer, therefore everyone that is godly pray to Him." God does hear prayer and because He hears it, we will call on Him as long as we live.

The Lord gives us another motive and keeps us praying by giving us constant needs. *"Give us this day our daily bread"* (Matt. 6:11). You might like to go and gather a week's worth of manna. It will stink before the end of the week. I like to have mine fresh every day. This is why everyone who is godly prays to God.

A Time

"Therefore let everyone who is godly offer prayer to you at a time when you may be found," or "in a time of finding." Is there a specific time when God is to be found? As long as you live and pray to God, He has promised to answer. Though it is the eleventh hour, do not hesitate to pray. Jesus said, *"The one who seeks finds"* (Matt. 7:8). If you truly seek Him, He will be found by you.

But there are also special times for finding God, like when His Spirit is poured out or when we realize our sin. The time when you will find out sin is the time when you will find God. When your eyes are blinded with tears of repentance, you will see the Savior clearly.

A time of decision is also a time for finding God. He has promised that if we seek Him with our whole hearts, He will be found by us. So, it will be when you come to God in full submission.

When the whole heart is determined to seek Jesus, then the Lord will come quickly and be found, especially when our trust is completely in the Lamb of God who takes away the sin of the world. You will find that God has found you when you are done with yourself and taken the blood and righteousness of Jesus to be the only hope of your soul.

Daily Reflection

There are ways to know and see if someone is godly: the fruits in their lives, their conduct, and the spiritual power they carry with them. But, we often overlook prayer as a measuring tool.

1. How would you describe a godly person?
2. Do you see yourself as godly?
3. What is the difference between the intensity and quantity of prayer?
4. Of the motives listed, which ones motivate you the most in prayer?
5. What does it mean to "find God"?

25

HUMILITY, THE FRIEND OF PRAYER

"I am not worthy of the least of all the deeds of steadfast love and all the faithfulness that you have shown to your servant, for with only my staff I crossed this Jordan, and now I have become two camps"
Genesis 32:10

It Is an Attitude of Prayer

Jacob could not have prayed unless he had stripped off the self-justification and stood naked before God. He was not talking to Laban, who he had slaved for, and who had taken advantage of him, but confessed to God, *"I am not worthy."*

If you want to say something about your own integrity and efforts, or if you have heard others speak your praise, forget it all, because you cannot pray if it has any effect on you. You cannot pray with a good opinion of yourself and say, *"God, I thank you that I am not like other men"* (Luke 18:11)—that is no prayer at all. God drives all proud prayers out of His temple.

"I am not worthy," should be our cry. Like Abraham, we acknowledge that we are dust and ashes, less than the least of all saints. It was right for Jacob, when he lifted his eyes to heaven, to use humble language. It would be wrong to use words of merit before God, for we have no merit, and if we had any, we would not need to pray. Jacob was afraid and distressed, and when a person is brought low, the humblest words suit them. Those who are filled with bread can boast, but the hungry beg.

We often fail in our prayers because we do not get low enough. If you have any righteousness of your own, you will never have Christ's righteousness. But when you can truly confess your nothingness, and lie low before God, He must hear you. *"Out of the depths I cry to you, O Lord!"* (Psalm 130:1). No prayers rise quicker than those that come from the depths.

Jacob does not say, "I **was** not worthy" but he says *"I am not worthy."* He believes that he was unworthy when he crossed the Jordan, but even now, looking upon his flocks, herds, family, and all that he had done, he cries *"I am not worthy!"*

He showed humility in confessing God's hand in his prosperity—*"all the deeds of steadfast love and all the faithfulness that you have shown to your servant."* Did he not breed those flocks himself? Wasn't it his own shrewd skills that made him wealthy? No, he speaks of it all as love and faithfulness which the Lord had shown to His servant. When we remember the steadfast love of the Lord to us, we can only acknowledge the contrast of our littleness with the greatness of His love and feel a sense of humiliation. It is written, *"They shall fear and tremble because of all the good and all the prosperity I provide"* (Jer. 33:9). No man could ever think that he deserved that the Son of God should die for him!

That which made Jacob humble, also made him strong in prayer.

It Is an Argument in Prayer

The first argument is that *"I am not worthy of the least of all."* Since God was gracious to Jacob when he was unworthy, he could stand while he wrestled with God. We are always afraid in our time of trouble that God will deal with us according to our unworthiness, but He will not. Is there not power in such a prayer?

Notice that while Jacob pleads his own unworthiness, he also pleads God's goodness. *"Steadfast love and all the faithfulness"*—these two go hand-in-hand in Jacob's prayer. If you want to wrestle with God and succeed, use these two master arguments; they are keys that open all the treasures of God, two shields to guard you against every fiery arrow.

Notice also how he says *"your servant,"* not *"your child"* or *"your chosen."* It might be a small thing to be a servant, but it is a great thing to plead in times of need, so David also used it: *"Make your face shine on your servant"* (Psalm 31:16); *"Hide not your face from your servant; for I am in distress"* (Psalm 69:17).

Jacob had another plea that showed his humility, and that was the argument of facts. With *"my staff I crossed this Jordan."* He contrasts his present condition and his two camps with that day of poverty when he first fled across the river. This retrospect humbled him, but it was a strength to him in prayer.

We have obtained, through our Lord Jesus and His Spirit, blessings so large that we are not worthy of the least of all these mercies. Shall we not use them to God's glory? Yes, more than ever, for we are determined to pray more, believe more, work more, and be more full of courage for the name and the truth of Jesus to be made known wherever our voice can be heard.

Daily Reflection

Humility is one of those aspects of Christianity that we agree with but have little idea of attaining, or we go about it the wrong way. To see it linked so closely to prayer shows us that it is possible to be humble as we pray. The key, as always, is our heart before God.

1. What does it mean to you, to say "I am not worthy"?
2. What does this statement mean: "No man could ever think that he deserved that the Son of God should die for him!"?
3. List the arguments. Which one is the easiest for you to use, and which is the hardest?
4. Read 2 Chronicles 7:14. How does this relate?

26

INTERCESSORY PRAYER

"And the Lord restored the fortunes of Job, when he had prayed for his friends"
Job 42:10

Intercessory prayer was the turning point for Job's restoration. When his heart began to expand in a prayer for his friends, then the heart of God showed itself by returning his prosperity to him. Let us learn to imitate the example of Job and pray for our friends, and perhaps we shall be restored.

There are many examples in the Bible of people praying for others. Abraham pleaded for his son Ishmael, and for Sodom. Moses prayed for the Israelites, and Solomon prayed for the assembled people. Jeremiah's tears were prayers for the nation.

Look at the disciples, remember how Peter prays on the top of the house and Stephen while he was stoned. Or Paul, *"remembering you in my prayers"* (Eph. 1:16). He also asks for prayer when he says *"pray for us"* (2 Thess. 3:1). And James says, *"pray for one another,"* and adds the privilege *"that you may be healed"* (James 5:16), as if the healing is not just for the sick, but to us who offer the prayer.

And, of course, Jesus, our example. Did anyone intercede as He did? Remember that golden prayer of His, where he cried for His own people, *"Keep them from the evil one"* (John 17:15). And even during the crucifixion, He was still an intercessor for others. *"Father, forgive them, for they know not what they do"* (Luke 23:34).

Intercessory prayer is very powerful; it has stopped plagues, removed the darkness over Egypt, healed diseases, and been instrumental in saving many souls. But, perhaps you doubt about interceding for someone who has fallen far into sin. Maybe you say, "I cannot pray for others, for I am so weak and powerless."

The success of prayer does not depend on the strength of the person who prays, but on the power of the argument they use. If you sow seed, you may be very weak, but it is not your hand that puts the seed into the ground which produces the harvest—it is the life and energy in the seed. It is the same in the prayer of faith.

In the case of Job, he prayed for his offending friends. They had spoken harshly of him, accused him of hypocrisy, and thought he was selfish. But Job comes to the mercy seat, and pleads that his friends may be accepted, too. Do not do that, however, in a threatening way. Do not carry your friends who are wrong to the discussion room or the debating club, but before God.

Job's three friends could not pray for themselves, because the Lord said He would not accept them if they did. He was angry with them, but for Job, He said, *"My servant Job shall pray for you, for I will accept his prayer"* (Job 42:8). There are many Christians who cannot pray; doubt has come in, sin has taken away their confidence, and they are so despondent that they cannot pray with faith. Besides, there are millions of sinners who are dead in sin, and they cannot pray—pray for them, it is a blessed thing.

How were you born again? It was because somebody else prayed for you. Your mothers' prayers fell hot while you were still little children. There are husbands who owe their conversion to their wives' prayers, brothers who must acknowledge that it was a sister's pleading, and children who must confess that their Sunday school teachers prayed for them. Now, if by others' prayers you and I came to Jesus, how can we repay this Christian kindness but by pleading for others?

Intercede for others, for how can you be Christians if you do not? Christians are priests, but not if they offer no sacrifice? Christians are lights, but not unless they shine for others? Christians are sent into the world, as Jesus was, but not unless they are sent to pray? Christians are not only meant to be blessed themselves, but through them, all the earth will be blessed, but how if you refuse to pray?

Mothers, bring your children before God! Fathers, carry your sons and your daughters! Let us take a wicked world and the dark places and cry aloud until God establishes and makes His church a praise in the earth.

Daily Reflection

We spend a lot of our prayer time praising God, thanking Him, bringing our requests, confessing, and focusing on our troubles and needs. Most times, we neglect to pray for others or add them in at the end of our prayers like an addendum. But we can see here that it was important in the lives of many Biblical characters, Jesus among them.

1. Do you find it easy to intercede for others? Why?
2. What does Spurgeon mean when he says, "The success of prayer does not depend on the strength of the person who prays, but on the power of the argument they use"?
3. Can you think of a time someone else prayed for you? What happened?
4. Can you remember any instances where you have prayed for someone else and seen an answer?

27

TRUE PRAYER—TRUE POWER!

"Therefore I say unto you, What things soever ye desire, when ye pray, believe that ye receive them, and ye shall have them"
Mark 11:24 (KJV)

How many people complain that they do not enjoy prayer? We are on our knees, but there is no sweet fellowship with God. There are many Christians that pray because they must pray and it is their duty, not because it is a wonderful thing to be allowed to draw near to God.

In the verse, Jesus speaks of things—**"What things** soever ye desire." He did not expect us to pray when we have nothing to pray for.

Christians should be able to answer the question, *"What is your wish? It shall be granted you. And what is your request?"*

(Esther 5:6). Imagine an archer shooting with his bow, and not knowing where the target is! Or a ship on a voyage, setting off without the captain having any idea of what he was looking for! In everything else, you have a plan. You will find it more helpful to your prayers if you have some objects to aim at or people to mention.

When you pray to Him, tell Him what you want. Don't ransack the Bible to find words to express yourself, but those that naturally come to you. Pray in your own words. Speak plainly to God, ask at once for what you want.

Another qualification of prayer is desire—"*What things soever ye **desire**.*" It is not prayer unless there are desires, needs, and wants. We must have such a desire for the thing we want, that we will not rise until we have it—but in submission to His will. No wonder God has not blessed us, because we are not passionate in prayer as we should be. We must be sincere; otherwise, we have no right to hope that the Lord will hear our prayer.

But, these two things would not succeed if they were not mixed with a still more essential and divine quality—faith in God. "***Believe*** *that ye receive them.*" You cannot pray unless you believe that God really hears and will answer you.

Do you believe in the power of prayer? There are a great many Christians who do not. They think it is a good thing, and they believe that sometimes it does wonders, but they do not think that real prayer is always successful.

God has promised to hear prayer and He will perform His promise. When you can plead His promise then your will is

His will. When I have faith and can plead the promise with sincere desire, it is no longer a question if I will get the blessing or not, or whether my will shall be done. Unless God deviates from His Word, *"we know that we have the requests that we have asked of him"* (1 John 5:15).

And now to go one step higher, together with definite objects, passionate desires, and strong faith in powerful prayer, there should be a realizing expectation—*"believe that ye **receive** them, and ye shall **have** them."*

We need a realizing assurance in prayer. To count the blessings before they come! To be sure that they are coming! To act as if we had them! When you have asked for your daily bread, do not worry about it anymore, but believe that God has heard you, and will give it to you. When you have taken your sick child before God to believe that the child will recover, or if it does not, that it will be a greater blessing to you and more glory to God, and so to leave it to Him.

Take your smallest trials before Him. He is a God that hears prayer, He acts not on common sense, but upon something higher than common sense—on uncommon faith. He cannot and He will not let the person who trusts Him be ashamed or confused.

These are the four essentials of prevailing, successful, and effective prayer—*"**What things** soever ye **desire**, when ye pray, **believe** that ye **receive** them, and ye shall **have** them."*

Daily Reflection

Spurgeon's ability to dissect verses and bring out deep meaning from phrases and words is incredible. By pulling this well-known scripture that we know so well, and then piecing it back together again, he brings insight and revelation to us. What seemed so simple now becomes an entire vault of information.

1. Can you answer the questions that Spurgeon puts forward:

- Do you enjoy prayer?
- *What is your wish?*
- Do you believe in the power of prayer?

2. Read Mark 11:24 again. Do you struggle with any part of it?

3. What do you think of the statement: "He will not let the person that trusts Him be ashamed or confused"?

28

THE POWER OF JESUS' NAME

"And his name—by faith in his name—has made this man strong whom you see and know, and the faith that is through Jesus has given the man this perfect health in the presence of you all"
Acts 3:16

This miracle happened because of the name of Jesus. Twice is it mentioned: *"And his name—by faith in his name."* We can see whose name it is in verse 6: *"But Peter said, "... In the name of Jesus Christ of Nazareth, rise up and walk!"*

The first name mentioned by Peter is *'Jesus.'* Jesus signifies Savior. In that name Jesus is omnipotence. The same power that made all worlds lies hidden in that name. The power that will raise the dead, and make new heavens and a new earth, is in that name, saving this world from all its sin.

Next, consider the name which follows, *'Christ.'* "The Messiah" was probably the term Peter used, and it was the title they would recognize. The Sent One, the believing Hebrews called him—the Anointed One, we like to call him now. We see at once what wonderful power dwells in Jesus when we connect him with his mission from God. He was no amateur Savior, but was commissioned by the Father, and received all that was necessary for the accomplishment of the work he was sent to perform.

The other title, *"Jesus Christ of Nazareth,"* seems to bring the Savior—the Anointed One—into the most intimate connection with humanity. He was truly man, *"bone of my bones and flesh of my flesh"* (Gen. 2:23). Though he came down and was lower than the angels for the suffering of death, God has exalted him and crowned him with glory and honor.

The name of *"Jesus Christ of Nazareth"* not only made demons tremble, and cry out, but it cast them out of those whom they had tormented. As the name of Jesus had power with devils, so it had power also with men. All forms of sickness yielded to that name. The name of Jesus is indeed mighty, for it has power with God himself. The name of *"Jesus Christ of Nazareth"* is full of power.

Use this name and nothing can stand before you. When we draw near to God, what is our strength to succeed in prayer? Is it not that we ask in the name of Jesus? If you leave out the name of Jesus, what are your prayers but sounding brass and a tinkling cymbal? Prayer without the name of Jesus has no wings to fly up to God. This is that golden ladder we use to climb up to the Throne of God and take precious things out of the hand of God. That name succeeds with God concerning everything and so enables us to succeed with man.

Now, was it the name of Christ, or was it faith in that name that healed the lame man? It says, *"And his name—by faith in his name—has made this man strong."* And then it adds: *"and the faith that is through Jesus has given the man this perfect health in the presence of you all,"* as if to put the crown on the head of faith rather than on the name of Christ. Faith always crowns Christ, and therefore Christ crowns faith. *"Your faith has saved you"* (Luke 7:50), said Christ to the woman who was a sinner. "No," someone says, "it was Christ who saved her." That is true; but Christ said that it was her faith that saved her, and he knew. So, here, it was the name of Christ that caused the miracle, but it was brought through faith in that name.

Whose faith was it? It was the faith of all three. I believe that, first, it was the faith of Peter and John. But, this man would not have been healed if it had not been for his own faith. He did not receive the blessing and then have a dead, cold heart about it; but he began at once to praise the Lord.

We never hold faith correctly except when we see Jesus as the center of it.

Daily Reflection

We often add the name of Jesus to the end of our prayer, and it becomes like the Amen. Something we say to show we are finished, or out of respect to God. But do we actually take cognizance of the power and glory of the name and understand why we should use it in prayer?

1. Do you ever pray the words: "in Jesus' name"? Why?
2. Do you think there is any connection between this and Exodus 20:7?
3. What do you understand by the statement: "Use this name and nothing can stand before you"?
4. Why is Jesus' name so effective with God?

29

JESUS' PRAYER AND PLEA

"Preserve me, O God, for in you I take refuge"
Psalm 16:1

In considering these words as Jesus' prayer, we see a perfect example that we might imitate Him.

In Hebrew, the first part of the verse translates as, "Preserve me, O Eli." That is one of the names of God, and the same name that Jesus used when he cried, *"Eli, Eli, lema sabachthani?" that is, "My God, my God, why have you forsaken me?"* (Matt. 27:46). The word 'Eli' can mean "The strong One." So, it is weakness crying to the Strong for strength: "Preserve me, you who are so strong, mighty, and uphold all things by the word of your power!" 'Eli' can also mean "The

Ever-Present One." "Ever-Present One, preserve me!" God is definitely "a very present help in trouble."

Next notice that this is prayed in a time of weakness. The person feels that he cannot preserve himself. Jesus was only weak because he had assumed our human nature, yet in his weakness there was no tendency to sin; but our weakness is linked with a continual liability to evil. So, if Jesus prayed, *"Preserve me, O God,"* how much more sincerely should we cry to the Lord?

This prayer appeals for a promised blessing. When the Savior prayed this prayer, he could remind his Father of the promise given through Isaiah (Isa. 49:7-8), and said to him, "You have said, 'I will preserve you' do as you have said, my Father!" Let us learn from this example, to plead the promises of God when we go to him in prayer. Praying without a promise is like going to war without a weapon.

Next, we see that this prayer of Jesus obtained an answer. He was preserved as a child from the jealousy of Herod and was delivered from those who wanted to kill Him. He was also preserved from falling into those who tried to entrap him in his words. He was like a doctor in a hospital full of lepers, yet never got sick.

Let us now turn to the plea that Jesus urged in support of his prayer: *"Preserve me, O God, for in you I take refuge."* In faith, He is a perfect example to us. As a man, Jesus used this plea to shelter from all evil under the Godly wings of power, wisdom, goodness, and truth.

Look carefully at the argument in Jesus' plea: *"Preserve me, O God, for in you I take refuge."* As God, He felt the power of that plea, so he knew that his Father would also feel its power. Jesus never forgot that the rule of the kingdom is, *"According to your faith be it done to you"* (Matt. 9:29). He knew that we must *"ask in faith, with no doubting, for the one who doubts is like a wave of the sea that is driven and tossed by the wind. For that person must not suppose that he will receive anything from the Lord"* (James 1:6-7). So, Jesus came to his Father with this plea, "I trust in you, I have absolute confidence in you, therefore, please preserve me." Can you say the same? Can you look up to God and say, *"In you I take refuge"*? If so, you may use it as Christ used it in pleading with his Father.

Before you sleep, pray this prayer: *"'Preserve me, O God!'* Preserve my body, family, house, from hurt or harm of every kind." Especially pray this in a spiritual sense: "Preserve me from the world; do not let me be carried away with its excitements, bow before its flattery, or fear its disapproval. Preserve me from the devil; do not let him tempt me more than what I am able to bear. Preserve me from myself; keep me from growing envious, selfish, proud, or lazy. Preserve me from evils known and from evils unknown."

May God give us the ability to pray this prayer, and to use the plea, *"Preserve me, O God, for in you I take refuge,"* for Jesus' sake! Amen.

Daily Reflection

This is a startling prayer, especially when we consider that they are attributed to Jesus. They are spoken in times of distress, a cry for help. It is freeing to know that if our Lord suffered and cried out, then it is alright for us to do the same, without shame.

1. Why is it important to appeal for a promised blessing?
2. What is the importance of praying with a promise?
3. What is the argument used in this prayer?
4. We often use this prayer for our physical well-being. Why is it more important for our spiritual lives?

30

LABORING FOR SOULS

"For as soon as Zion was in labor she brought forth her children"
Isaiah 66:8

It is clear from the verse that there must be a time of labor before spiritual birth. To sincerely desire that God will give a large spiritual blessing to His church, there must be a time of labor and suffering. Before a great blessing comes on God's people, it has been preceded by great searchings of heart.

Before God began to work setting His people free from Egypt, He made them begin to cry. Their sighs and cries came up to God and He stretched out His hand to deliver them. The whole nation cried, and this labor and suffering brought its result.

Look at the yearnings David had. What requests he poured out for God to visit Zion, and make the vine which He had planted flourish once again. Even when his own sins were heavy on him, he could not end his personal confession without begging the Lord to build the walls of Jerusalem. There was a lot of heart labor in Israel and Judah, and the result was that the Lord was glorified, and belief in Him flourished.

Remember Josiah, the king. His heart was ready to break with anguish because of the suffering his people would have to endure on account of their sins. Then a glorious reformation came, which purged the land of idols and caused the Passover to be observed as never before. Labor of heart among the godly produced the change.

Look at the disciples in the upper room, waiting with anxious hope. Every heart there had been plowed with anguish by the death of the Lord. Each one was intended to receive the promised benefit of the Spirit. There, with one heart and one mind, they waited, but not without wrestling prayer, and so the Comforter was given, and three thousand people were born again.

Luther was not the only man to bring about the Reformation. There were hundreds who sighed and cried in secret. There were hearts breaking for the Lord to appear in miraculous ways.

We see this in the life of Jesus. He is the Savior of men, but before He could save others, He learned to sympathize with them. He wept over Jerusalem. He sweated great drops of blood in Gethsemane. As the Captain of our salvation, in bringing many to glory, He was made perfect by suffering. He did not go out to preach until He had spent nights in intercessory prayer, filled with strong cries and tears for the salvation of those who would hear. It is only when our heart breaks to see men saved that we will see sinners' hearts broken. The secret of success lies in passionate labor and suffering for souls.

Do you wish for your children's conversion? You will see them saved when you agonize for them. Many parents who have been privileged to see their child walking in the truth will tell you that before the blessing came, they had spent many hours in prayer, pleading with God. And then the Lord visited the child and renewed their heart.

It is the order of nature. The child is not born into the world without the sorrows of the mother; the bread that sustains life is not harvested from the earth without work and labor. *"By the sweat of your face you shall eat bread"* (Gen. 3:19), was a part of the curse. As it is in the natural, so is it in the spiritual. There will be no blessing without first sincerely yearning for it. If there is no labor, there will be no profit.

These times of labor produce grateful love for God. They test our faith in the power of God to save others. They drive us to the mercy seat. They strengthen our patience and perseverance, and every character in us is educated and increased.

Usually, when God intends to bless a church, it will begin in this way—two or three of the people are worried about what they see and become troubled in their hearts. The passion to see the church revived takes hold of them. They suffer anguish and sorrow in their hearts for sinners. They labor in birth for souls.

There is no greater joy, except the joy of our own relationship with Jesus than that of bringing others to trust the Savior.

Daily Reflection

We understand we should pray for others, but often we stop short of actually laboring over their souls, crying out for them. It seems to be another level that we need to attain if we want to see breakthroughs in people's lives—to see revival.

1. Have you ever agonized and labored in prayer for someone? What happened?
2. Why does God require this of us in order to see revival and results?
3. Do you have a heart for the lost?
4. Read Matthew 28:19-20. What is our part in this Great Commission?

31

THE AMEN

"The words of the Amen, the faithful and true witness, the beginning of God's creation"
Revelation 3:14

The word 'Amen' means "true, faithful, and certain," but its sense will be better seen by looking at three forms of its practical meaning.

First, it was used in asserting that when a person would give authority to his words, he either began or ended with the word Amen, to mean "certainly, assuredly, so it is." Jesus used the term often. The translated word "Truly, truly," is the word 'Amen.'

The second sense of the word 'Amen' can be described as consenting. An example of this is the people on Mount Ebal and Gerizim, when the curses and blessings were read out, they said "Amen, amen." So it will be.

A third meaning of the word Amen is petitionary. In this sense, we use it at the end of our prayers. "Our Father who art in heaven" is not a complete example of public prayer until it concludes with "Amen." In the early church, it was customary for everyone to say Amen.

In each of these, Jesus is certainly "the Amen." He asserts the will of God—the Son is the Word who asserts, declares, and testifies God. Secondly, Jesus consents to the will, design, and purpose of God. He gives an Amen to the will of God—is the echo, in His life and His death, of the eternal purposes of the Most High. And thirdly, He is "the Amen" in the petitionary sense; for all our prayers He gives them force and power.

Jesus is "the Amen" in reference to God, "the Amen" as viewed in Himself, and "The Amen" in regard to ourselves.

Jesus Is God's Amen

If God had not decided to give Jesus to be a Redeemer, the purpose of redemption would have had no Amen. If He had not appointed Him to be the head of the body, His purpose concerning the body would have lacked the Amen. That gift of Jesus to us in the eternal covenant was the Father stamping His decree and making it valid and good.

He was God's Amen to His eternal purpose.

When Jesus came on the earth, He was God's Amen to the long line of prophecies and the Amen to all the Levitical types. The sacrifices offered by Aaron and his sons were only a symbol; they lacked the Amen to give it body, force, and substance. When Jesus went to the cross, God solemnly put an Amen into what had been indefinite.

Jesus is God's Amen to all His covenant promises, for it is written that *"For all the promises of God find their Yes in him. That is why it is through him that we utter our Amen to God for his glory"* (2 Cor. 1:20). The gift of Jesus was God making every promise sure and certain.

Once more, Jesus will be God's Amen at the end of time. When He comes, the righteous will be rewarded, and the wicked will be condemned.

Jesus Is Amen in Himself

He proved Himself to be Amen, the God of truth, sincerity, and faithfulness, in His fulfillment of the covenant. He has paid the price to the full.

He was also "the Amen" in all His teachings and all His promises. Jesus is also Amen in all His offices as a priest to pardon and cleanse, a King to rule and reign, and a prophet to tell of good things to come.

He is Amen to His righteousness. He is Amen in every single title He has: your Husband, never seeking divorce; your Head, the neck never dislocated; your Friend, sticking closer than a brother; your Shepherd, with you in death's dark valley; your Help and your Deliverer; your Castle and your

High Tower; the horn of your strength, your confidence, your joy, your all in all, and Amen in all.

Jesus Is God's Amen to Every Christian

Jesus is the Amen in us. If you want to know God, you must know Jesus. If you want to be sure of the truth of the Bible, you must believe in Jesus. And when you have seen Him bearing your sins, and have felt the joy and peace that flow from believing in God, you will have heard an Amen to the Bible, and an Amen to the existence of God, and an Amen to the Gospel.

Next, Jesus is "the Amen" for us. When you pray, you say Amen. Did you think of Jesus? Did you look at His scars? Did you offer your prayer through Him? Did you ask Him to present it before God? Did you expect to be heard by virtue of His intercession? If not, there is no Amen to your prayer. But if you have prayed, looking to the Cross, Jesus Christ's blood said Amen, and your prayer is certain to be heard in heaven.

I want Jesus to be God's Amen in all our hearts, for all the good things of the covenant He will be if you receive Him. If you have Jesus, you have entered into rest. *"Justified by faith, we have peace with God"* (Rom. 5:1). If you have Jesus, you are saved. He is God's Amen.

Daily Reflection

How many times do we glibly tack on the word 'Amen' to our prayers without even thinking of its significance and meaning? Most of us know that its ancient translation signifies that we are in agreement, but here, Spurgeon opens our eyes to see Jesus as the Amen!

1. What is your understanding of the word 'Amen' at the end of your prayer?
2. How is Jesus God's Amen? How is He Amen in Himself, and to us?
3. What significance should this bring to our prayers?
4. Is Jesus Amen in your life?

ABOUT C. H. SPURGEON

Charles Haddon Spurgeon was born in Essex in June 1834. Although he lived over 100 years ago, his name is still widely spoken as an admired and respected Christian writer and preacher. His books and sermons are read to this day.

Spurgeon grew up in a working-class house, where they were only able to afford local schooling for him. As a result of the average standard of education, he never went on to achieve a university degree. But, his love for books and learning continued well into his adult years, and at the time of his death, he had amassed a personal library of over 12,000 books.

His conversion happened during a sudden snowstorm when he was forced to take cover in a nearby church. After listening to the sermon, he was born again. Only 15 years old, Spurgeon was baptized a few days later and joined the local Baptist church.

His style and energy saw the pews fill up for every sermon that he preached, even though he was only a teenager. He was soon invited to New Park Street Chapel in London, where the congregation asked him to stay on. After some time there, he began traveling, often preaching to thousands at a time. Spurgeon's quick memory allowed him to speak without having to read from his sermon notes, and he often acted out passages or stories. But, some people criticized him for these antics, and it would be a constant thorn in his flesh.

"I am perhaps vulgar, but it is not intentional, save that I must and will make people listen. My firm conviction is that we have had enough polite preachers," he said in response to those who found his mannerisms a bit too much. His style was simple and direct, with many stories to give real-life examples, and many loved listening to him, which garnered him the title, "Prince of Preachers."

In 1861, he moved his congregation into the Metropolitan Tabernacle, a much larger premises that could seat up to 5,000 at a time. Baptism according to the Bible was always a strong point that he challenged people on, as well as the issue of slavery. He also managed to find time to open an orphanage and a pastors' college.

His health deteriorated, and he had to take time off in France after his doctors urged him to rest. He never fully improved and he stopped all his public duties. He passed away soon after in 1892, with a funeral that drew thousands of people who had heard him preach.

REFERENCES

Crossway. (2001). *English standard version Bible*. Crossway Bibles.

Thomas Nelson Publishers. (2014). *Holy Bible, KJV*. Thomas Nelson Pub.

www.ingramcontent.com/pod-product-compliance
Lightning Source LLC
LaVergne TN
LVHW010226070526
838199LV00062B/4745